Genesis of Grace

Genesis of Grace

A Lenten Book of Days

John Indermark

UPPER
ROOM BOOKS®
NASHVILLE

Cover design: Michele Wetherbee

Cover illustration: Douglas Andelin

Fourth printing: 2000

Library of Congress Cataloging-in-Publication
Indermark, John, 1950–
   Genesis of grace: a Lenten book of days / by John Indermark.
      p.   cm.
   ISBN 0-8358-0843-2
      1. Bible. O. T. Genesis—Study and teaching. 2. Lent—Prayer-books and devotions—English. I. Title.
   BS1239.I53   1998   97-9245
   222'.1106—dc21   CIP

To

Judy and Jeff

for believing and waiting . . .

and gracing

Contents

Foreword

THE OLD TESTAMENT IS LAW; the New Testament is grace. That misconception has plagued the church and Christian theology—not to mention Jewish-Christian relationships—for almost two millennia. The truth of the matter is that grace weaves its course throughout the Hebrew Scriptures, often coming to the fore at critical junctures.

Nowhere is that revelation clearer in the Hebrew Scriptures than in Genesis. This book of "beginnings" (as Genesis and its Hebrew parallel *beresit* literally mean) declares God's disposition toward humanity and creation to be a fundamentally gracious one. That is, God consistently does for us what we cannot do for ourselves or what we have done nothing to merit.

Genesis of Grace consists of daily reflective readings keyed to each of the days of Lent. These readings follow the weave of grace through the events and characters of Genesis. They intend to evoke meditation upon and recognition of the active presence of God's grace. Each week of readings centers around a common theme and character(s). While the readings vary in style and emphasis, their core purpose remains constant: to moor the gospel's declaration of God's grace for your life and mine within the foundational stories of Genesis. "In the beginning" not only witnesses to a God of creation but to a God of grace.

Some of you may be part of a Lenten study group that uses an accompanying leader's guide. Some of you may gather informally on occasion to discuss the readings and their implications during this season of Lent. Some of you may use this book exclusively as a personal devotional guide. This resource seeks to be of value in any of those contexts. However, giving adequate time to reflect on the texts and their readings is key to its purpose.

Traditionally we associate the days of Lent with discipline. Clear your daily schedule to provide the time, space, and quiet that will enhance your meditation upon these readings. It may be early morning before breakfast when no others stir, and the phone hasn't started ringing. It may be a nighttime "vesper" before sleep, a way of giving both body and spirit time to be still. It may be a midafternoon break from work or studies, a miniature "sabbath" you give yourself to freshen the day. You might even consider reading each day's text from Genesis and its accompanying reflection early in the day, then return to them at night. What occurred during the day that might relate to those readings? Do you hear anything new, having lived with them for a day?

Whatever pattern you employ to explore *Genesis of Grace*, enjoy it. Revisit the characters of Genesis with imagination and faith. Allow their humanity, as well as the unexpected ways grace transforms them, to surprise you. Listen to the reflections on the texts, allowing them to spur your own thoughts and feelings...your own remembrances of grace that delighted, challenged, and renewed you. And let these reflections on grace that move through our faith's book of beginnings accompany you on the Lenten journey that leads to Jerusalem and the cross—and beyond. One grace and one God are at work in creation and redemption. The same grace in Genesis that calls us to be heirs of the covenant's promises still calls us through Christ to be heirs of the covenant's hope.

Thanks be to the God of Genesis, who is the God of grace!

Acknowledgments

ONE TRANSLATION OF THE PRAYER OF JESUS counsels us to forgive our debts. In the case of this book, I would be remiss without acknowledging my debts to those who shaped this work. I ask forgiveness from those whom I unintentionally overlook.

My editor, George Donigian, has been a steady advocate for this project, encouraging my work with both freedom to explore anew the fields of Genesis and discipline to better state the grace to be gleaned therein. A word of appreciation is also owed to Rita Collett, who served as my first contact with Upper Room Books. Rita's editing on a prior curriculum project provided me with valuable experience in writing for publication, even as her copyediting on this manuscript sharpened both words and message. Glenda Webb's careful and helpful attention to details of accuracy and verification likewise merit my thanks.

The spark for this work and many of its approaches to specific texts came years ago when I read the commentary on Genesis written by Dr. Walter Brueggemann, who had earlier been my professor and advisor at Eden Theological Seminary. Dr. Brueggemann also connected me with Herbert Lambert, a former editor at the Christian Board of Publication, who offered helpful suggestions at an early stage of this work's prehistory.

As a parish pastor, I am indebted to the learnings of grace from individuals and communities of faith encountered along the way. In particular, the congregations of Tolt Congregational United Church of Christ, Naselle Congregational U.C.C., and Grays River United Methodist Church extended patient hearings of a sermon series on Genesis that formed the initial stirrings of this book's reflections. Long before, the teachers and ministers of Salvator Evangelical and Reformed Church (St. Louis) instilled a loving fascination for scripture that continues to energize me.

My appreciation also extends to a group of writers with whom I meet monthly for support and inspiration: Pat Thomas, Lorne Wirkkala, Jenelle Varila, Robert and Thea Pyle, Diane Matthews, and Sue Holway. They have listened and critiqued some of this book's material and generally have helped to hone my craft of writing over the past five or so years, though any fault for that honing's not being sharp enough rests with me, not them.

And finally, I owe thanks and far more to Judy and Jeff Indermark for allowing husband and father the gift of spending inordinate amounts of time before a computer screen in order to cultivate a ministry of the written word.

~⌒⊃

ASH WEDNESDAY

Genesis 1:26-27   **Fingerprints**

Then God said, "Let us make humankind in our image."

ASH WEDNESDAY. FOR A THOUSAND YEARS and more, ashes have marked the foreheads of persons entering the season of Lent. One tradition calls for the ashes to come from burning the palms of the previous year's Palm Sunday celebration. Another tradition calls for signing the forehead with ashes in the form of the cross. Yet another tradition calls for the recitation of Genesis 3:19*b* as the ashes are imposed: "You are dust, and to dust you shall return." Palm, cross, and dust. Joy, sacrifice, and penitence. All comingled in our imprinting with ashes.

No more than fifteen of us gathered in a circle on Ash Wednesday evening. In silence, by candlelight, I moved around the inside of the circle, marking foreheads with the mix of palm ash and water in the plate. Even in that dim light, I noticed a curious thing. If, in my final signing of the cross, I pressed steady with my thumb, I left my fingerprint within the cross.

Genesis 1:26-27 relates our being made in the image of God. Creation proceeds on this day as it did each day before. God's word begets God's creation. God's creation begets God's declaration of its goodness. No exceptions: "It was very good."

So what have traditions of Ash Wednesday and fingerprints on foreheads and the goodness of Genesis 1 to do with one another? God marks our lives with the fingerprints of grace.

The imagery of God's fingers at work in creation finds expression in Psalm 8:3, which declares that the heavens are "the work of your fingers." Consider the affirmation of Genesis 1:26 that we are created in God's image. We bear within ourselves the "imprint" of God's presence, the vocation of revealing that presence in creation.

Creation itself is an act of grace: Nothing compelled God to fashion life. Our creation as human beings reveals that grace even more profoundly. Nothing coerced God to fashion others in the divine image, with all the potential that image implies. The "fingerprints" of grace mark us from the beginning. And these fingerprints will continue to leave their traces upon those whose stories Genesis narrates, stories we will follow through Lent.

Some of you reading this devotion may well experience the imposition of ashes this day or evening. The penitential nature of that rite and of the service in which it occurs reminds us that we indeed have fallen short of serving as the image of God in creation. Foreheads are marked with the ashes of former joys, signed in the form of discipleship's cross.

But remember that in the ashes, other fingerprints may be seen: the fingerprint of grace bringing life, our lives, into being; the fingerprint of grace declaring human creation, our creation, to be "very good" (Gen. 1:31). Before anything else marks (or mars) our life, God's fingers leave the imprint of grace—an imprint that stamps us with the word of God's favor.

For Meditation This Day

God, forgive what causes me to lose sight of your grace. Mark my life anew with the imprint of your creative and forgiving touch.

Week One

Dust and Seeds

Thursday

Genesis 2:4-7   **Formed of Dust**

The Lord God formed man from the dust of the ground.

I T ALL BEGINS IN DUST. The creativity of an Amadeus
Mozart, the compassion of a Mother Teresa, the brilliance
of a Stephen Hawking, the faith of a young Nazarene
woman named Mary—all begotten of dust.

Dust even gave humanity its first name. In Hebrew, the
word for ground or earth is *'adamah*. Thus, in a subtle but
revealing play on words, God formed *'adam* (Adam) from the
dust of the *'adamah*. In the earthy imagery of Genesis, dust not
only describes what we are—dust christens who we are. *'Adam*.

Scientists hypothesize that some trace elements in our bodies come from the dust of stars born of creation's first explosive
light. The idea of such an origin surprises some. It shouldn't.
Genesis sees the same hand that flung galaxies into motion
and lit novas to blazing as shaping humankind out of dust.

Out of dust. The idea sounds so, well, ordinary. Might not
God have been better served by forming the blessed image-
creature with something a bit more noble, a bit more valuable?
To start from a fleck of gold would have been nice or a dollop
of crude oil. Perhaps then we might have valued one another
more highly, if for no other reason than to protect our inher-
ent market value.

But what is the value of dust? "Then the Lord God...
breathed into his nostrils the breath of life." It seems that the
value of dust, our value, derives from the breathing of God's
breath—into dust, into us. God would have had a hard time

16   GENESIS OF GRACE

finding anything more ordinary than dust. Yet into the ordinary, God breathes life.

And that becomes one of the very first clues in Genesis that grace defines the manner of this God toward creation. What of dust merited the gift of God's breath moistening its soiled bits into life? What of dust held the promise of birthing an infant's cry or harboring a parent's love? Such potential would be hard to discern, even if you put a speck of earth under the penetrating gaze of an electron microscope. But somehow, the breath of God fashioned ordinary dust into the living image of God.

We are formed of dust—which suggests, among other things, not only our humble beginnings but our startling potential. For if God can breathe life into soil, what does that say about the latent potential in our lives? Who can tell what God's breath might make of us yet—of will and mind, of imagination and compassion—opened to the One whose breath is life?

You are formed of dust, a child of God's creation. Think of the particular ways in which God graces your existence: with relationships, with faith, with love, with community. Add to that list those things (and persons) that trigger your gratitude. In each of those life-gracing gifts, God breathes life into you. Yet even those gifts do not exhaust your life's possibilities. Relationships can grow; faith can deepen; love can broaden; community can expand. The potential is there. God has breathed it into you.

You and I find our origins in the dust, but Genesis does not leave us there. God's grace enacted in creation invokes the promise of those formed from dust, the promise you carry within you—your potential to be the very image of God in this creation.

For Meditation This Day

You have fashioned me from dust, O God. Help me see your
hand and feel your breath in all the ordinary corners of my life,
that I may sense the extraordinary potential of your grace.

Friday

Genesis 2:18-22 **Helper**

"It is not good that the ['adam] should be alone."

THE HOLLOW STARE OF LONELINESS gazes even from the
garden. One might have assumed communion with God
to be enough for the one formed from dust, to say nothing
of us. Remarkably and selflessly, God determines it is not. "It
is not good" mimics God's pronouncement at the end of each
day in Genesis 1. Here in Genesis 2, the lack of goodness
betrays an unfinished act of creation. What remains for God
to fashion is human community.

Helper is the decisive word in this quest for what the *'adam*
lacks. In the second chapter of Genesis, contrary to the first,
this quest for companionship and community spurs the creation of all living things (except, curiously, the sea creatures).
But God finds the "helper" nowhere. Human community calls
for something—someone—new in creation.

Sleep falls; flesh opens. God takes part of the *'adam's* own
being to fashion this new creation. The story speaks little of
scientific origins and nothing of gender primacy but volumes
about relationship. "Adam's rib" is not a joke but a statement of
mutuality—how human life intertwines at its very core.

So God fashioned the helper of the *'adam*. For some today,

the word *helper* resonates with subservience: helper as in "little" or as a lackey. Such a presumptuous hearing does not do justice to the biblical use of the word. *Help* or *helper* (*ezer*) occurs twenty-one times in the Hebrew Scriptures. Two of these references occur in today's text from Genesis about the partner of the *'adam*. In the remaining nineteen occurrences, *ezer* refers either to the help God brings or to God as helper. "The God of my father was my help [*ezer*], and delivered me from the sword of Pharaoh" (Exod. 18:4). If we understand the term *ezer* as describing a subordinate, what does that make of the God who is the *ezer* of Israel, whose "help" includes deliverance from Egypt?

God's wisdom recognizes the loneliness of the human condition. God responds in love by creating the potential for community in the "helper." It is a rhythm as ancient as this Hebrew book of beginnings and as fresh as our own yearnings for companionship. And its rhythm reveals grace. In the need for community to stave off loneliness, God fashions another who bears the image of God.

And that truly is the gift of human relationship: to see in another human being one's own identity as a child of God and to provide for others that same window to their sacred identity. Alone, one is apt either to lose self-worth in despair or to inflate self-importance in arrogance. In community, we find help—and helpers—to maintain a faithful balance between those extremes.

"It is not good that the [*'adam*] should be alone." Some say that as much as things change, so also do things stay the same. Loneliness remains an adversary. Relationship remains an ally. And God's grace remains the source of community: the gift that reminds us we are not alone.

For Meditation This Day

You reach into my loneliness, O God, by touch of Spirit, by hand of family, by voice of friend. When I am tempted to withdraw into self, draw me into community that I may see your grace incarnate in the love and friendship of others.

⁓

Saturday

Genesis 3:1-13   **Hiding in Blame**

The man and his wife hid themselves.

ONE OF CHILDHOOD'S FIRST GAMES is hide-and-seek. One child counts while the rest scatter, hoping to conceal themselves from the searcher's sight. To succeed at hide-and-seek involves using whatever is near to draw attention away from one's own self and body. We learn the game early, perhaps because it becomes one we practice all our lives long. As the years mount, we simply grow more skillful in finding things—or others—to cover us.

Consider this text that tradition has christened "The Fall." The characters and plot hold no surprise: the serpent, the woman, the man, in order of appearance; the craftiness, the bite, the sharing, in order of action. For some, the story fast-forwards to the inevitable judgment. But hold that thought for now. Because at the moment, the Garden provides the setting for what may be the first recorded incident of hide-and-seek, though not the last by any means.

In truth, two games of hiding take place. The first and most obvious comes when the man and the woman conceal themselves among the trees. Perhaps God smiled at this effort, the way a parent might at a young child who huddles behind a leafless bush or inside an open-topped box. The second hiding, however, possesses no lightness of spirit. When God inquires of the man why he ate from the tree of which he had been commanded not to eat, the man's reply scrambles to give cover: "The *woman* whom *you* gave to be with me, *she* gave me fruit from the tree." When God questions the woman about her action, her response seeks the same distancing of self from responsibility: "The *serpent* tricked me."

In other words, once the trees prove inadequate for cover, blame of others becomes the preferred means of hiding. And if the truth be told, which is after all the intent of these stories, blame of others has been our favorite hiding place ever since. The litany rings familiar, with all manner of variations: It's not my fault....I was only following orders....If she hadn't been dressed like that....If he had only minded his own business. Perhaps you can add your own.

Hiding our words and actions in the blame of others is an old game, if we trust the story from Genesis. In the end, such hiding is no more viable than turning our bodies sideways in the hope that a fence post will shield us. Why? We cannot hide from God. Genesis 3 reveals the folly of such an attempt in story form. Psalm 139 does the same in its poetry. "Where can I go from your spirit?" it asks. Heaven, Sheol, the place of the sun's rising and its setting, lightness and darkness—the psalm offers all as prospective escapes, but none proves adequate. "You hem me in, behind and before, / and lay your hand upon me." Such is God's presence.

Besides its futility, hiding in the blame of others creates an insidious dilemma. As long as a person avoids responsibility or culpability, he or she holds at arm's length the grace to heal, forgive, and renew. The man finds it difficult to ask for forgiveness when he says the woman's to blame. The woman has difficulty asking for forgiveness when she says it's the serpent's doing. Hiding in blame only obscures our view of grace.

Yet grace clings with surprising tenacity. Even after Eden's couple chooses the path of disobedience, even when they do their best to hide themselves from God's presence, God seeks them out. The grace of God in Genesis proves as persevering as the presence of God in Psalm 139. No matter how we try to hide or distance ourselves, God comes, God finds, and God graces our lives.

For Meditation This Day
Do not let me hide from you, O God, lest I think I might succeed. Keep me from using the wrongs of others, real or perceived, to camouflage my own wrongs, for I need not distraction but grace.

Sunday

Genesis 3:14-19   **Seed of Hope**

"I will put enmity...between thy seed and her seed; it shall bruise thy head, and thou shalt bruise his heel." (KJV)

HAVING EATEN THE FRUIT of the one forbidden tree, the man and woman reap a bitter harvest. Disobedience bears consequences. Some of those consequences, summarized in the judgments levied by God, offer explanations for physical peculiarities in the world. The serpent slithers on its stomach. The woman bears children in pain. The man sweats in order to eat. The earth produces thorns and thistles as well as grains and fruits.

Other consequences run deeper. The enmity between the offspring of the serpent and the woman finds expression in the innate human aversion to snakes. The subordination of wife to husband issues from creation's corruption, not its original goodness where male and female share both God's image and blessing equally (1:27-28). The vocation to till the garden plummets into the drudgery of toiling on profaned ground. Adam, the one formed of dust, has brought down God's curse upon the ground. Life will never be the same.

To this point, the story reads in an uncomfortably familiar manner. Bad choices beget bad results. Worse yet, those results too often impact innocents outside the circle of guilt. What had the ground done to warrant the repercussions of disobedience by the one drawn from it? Then again, what do victims struck head-on by the car of a drunk driver do to deserve being caught in the wake of another's folly? The sin of one remains a leading cause of pain and suffering in blameless others.

Perhaps God should have literally kept the forewarned promise concerning the price of disobedience: "In the day that you eat of it you shall die." Notice that God doesn't say, "You shall die symbolically." Nor does God say, "You shall die spiritually." No, "you shall die" is the word.

If God's sole concern were righteous judgment, then maybe that's what would have happened: a clean slate, a fresh start. But the God of Genesis chooses to be a God of grace. God acts here much as a parent might when confronted with a child's serious offense. First thoughts might suggest severe consequences that will insure "never again." But one can never guarantee such insurance, and severity may contradict love. So while punishment and discipline may follow, the relationship between parent and child does not end. God has invested too much love in forging that bond.

The analogy is not perfect, but it does provide a way of understanding God's action in Genesis 3. Enmity and pain will follow without doubt. But because God does not levy death, there will be life. And as long as there is life, hope endures.

Hope emerges in the midst of these judgments in the form of a seed. While recent translations render the Hebrew word in verse 15 as "offspring," the King James Version retains the literal translation of "seed." On the surface, the verse may offer little consolation: Bad blood will exist between the serpent's and the woman's progeny. In later Jewish and then Christian tradition, however, the words take on messianic overtones. The "bruising" of the serpent's head suggests that one of the woman's seed will crush the consequences of Eden's disobedience. Likewise, the bruising of the heel insinuates that disobedience will carry a cost to the woman's seed. Perhaps Luke's tracing the genealogy of Jesus to "son of Adam" echoes that ancient hope.

In ground cursed by disobedience, God sows a seed of hope. Maybe you have experienced the grace of God's not giving up on you so easily. Remember that experience when you feel like giving up on another—or yourself. You bear that seed within you.

For Meditation This Day
Too often, O God, I speak or act without taking thought of the consequences. And when those consequences sometimes fall hard on me, I forget about hope—and grace—and you. Help me remember.

Monday

Genesis 4:1-7   **Seed of Tragedy**

The Lord had regard for Abel and his offering,
but for Cain and his offering he had no regard.

FAVORITISM. HAVE YOU EVER BEEN its victim or its beneficiary? Can you remember that one classmate who
always seemed to catch the teacher's praise, while you
knew you worked just as hard but never got the recognition?
Or perhaps the tension struck closer to home: A sibling seemingly could do no wrong (or right) in your parents' eyes. Of
course, adulthood does not end such perceived bias for or
against us. You have known favoritism to rear its head in the
workplace or among friends—or in your attitude toward former and current pastors and parishioners.

When we receive favor, we may chalk it up to our good fortune or even our just rewards. When we are "left out" of such
favor, we may grow angry or resentful—not just toward the
one showing favor but toward the favored one.

If you have found yourself on both sides of the favor issue
at one time or another, it will better prepare you to understand
the tug of emotions at play in the story of Cain and Abel. It is
the first, but not the last, of the brother stories in Genesis.
And, as if to preface the struggles ahead, a crucial wedge jeop-
ardizes the relationship between Cain and Abel. The wedge
owes its creation not to parents or siblings but to God. "[God]
had regard for Abel and his offering, but for Cain and his
offering God had no regard." The text does not explain the
difference in regard. One finds favor; the other does not.

With whom do you identify: the "fair-haired" Abel, the "star-crossed" Cain—or perhaps the God whose decision spawns an outcome that looms uncomfortably close? For Abel, God's favor is gracious. For Cain, God's favor is capricious. For God, favor springs from autonomy: I will be gracious to whom I will.

Grace need not cause tragedy; yet that is how the story unfolds. Cain grows angry. (Be honest now, wouldn't you?) Notice that God does not respond with "Don't be angry," as if Cain's anger is unfounded. Instead, God proposes a question: "Why are you angry?" Why? Because of your bad fortune or your brother's good fortune? If it's the latter, hope remains: "If you do well, will you not be accepted?" The aim of the sacrificial system is to attain God's acceptance. Cain can reverse his ill-fortune. But if Cain's anger focuses on Abel, tragedy impends: "If you do not do well, sin is lurking at the door."

What is on the other side of that door for Cain and Abel awaits tomorrow's reading. But for today, the story of God's favor and these brothers suffices to teach an important lesson. For reasons beyond our comprehension, life is not always fair. We bask in God's grace when it falls fresh on us; sometimes we grow anxious and resentful when it misses us and descends inexplicably on others.

God allows us wide berth for baring our struggles and our "how longs" to God. Tragedies arise when we turn our envy against those we deem to have received our due unfairly. "Why are you angry?" God asked Cain—and God asks us. What will we do with our anger? The answer awaits our living.

For Meditation This Day
Guide me, O God, when you seem distant or when life's unfairness overwhelms. Help me rejoice in others' well-being, rather than resent their good fortune. Lead me to grace that accepts, loves, and embraces me as I am.

Tuesday

Genesis 4:8-12   **When Dust Cries Out**

*"Listen; your brother's blood is crying out
to me from the ground."*

I REMEMBER A SUBSTITUTE TEACHER in grade school who once baffled everyone in class with a cockeyed theory about sound and objects. Since sound consists of physically detectable waves and since all objects are more or less porous at the atomic level, objects potentially could absorb all sounds within their "hearing." And what if someone invented an instrument that extracted and reproduced all the sound waves once absorbed in those objects? A stone from the Acropolis in Athens might release the voice of Aristotle. A sedimentary layer deep in the Grand Canyon might air the braying of dinosaurs. A chunk of asteroid might echo with the whispers of space.

Of course, such ideas belong to childhood fantasies. Stones can no more harbor sounds than ground can give them voice....

Cain called Abel out to the field and killed him. No glamour attaches to the murder as described in Genesis. All that prefaces it is Cain's anger and God's warning of sin that lurks. Suddenly, it is Cain who lurks while God wonders as to the whereabouts of sin's newest victim.

Curious, isn't it, that God asks where Abel is. Did God not see the violence? Sometimes life seems very much like that. Was God's head turned when the rice fields of Cambodia became its killing fields? Is God preoccupied when children fall victim to predators of all ages? Perhaps those who do the violence, like Cain, hope it is so, hope that there are no witnesses.

Certainly, Cain offers no help: "I do not know; am I my brother's keeper?"

Then the totally unexpected happens: One witness speaks up—the blood of one son from Adam cries out against the other son of Adam. The voice wells up from the ground (*'adamah*)! The ground, from which God drew and named human life, now raises its voice to condemn that life's taking. The stones can talk: if only we would listen, if only we would learn.

In 1988 my family walked on the grounds of what had been the Bergen-Belsen concentration camp in Germany. None of the original structures remained. A small museum area displayed maps, pictures, and statistics. But far more evocative of that place were scattered mounds of earth faced with gray stone-block walls. HIER RUHEN 5,000 TOTE, said an engraving on one set of the blocks (translated as "Here lie 5,000 dead" or "Here rest 5,000 of the dead"). Other inscriptions differed from that simple formula only in the number given: 5,000; 3,000...by now I have forgotten the total number. But I have not forgotten the mounded, grass-covered ground. It spoke with utter eloquence.

"Listen; your brother's blood is crying out to me from the ground!" I used to think that the author of Genesis wrote figuratively here. Now I'm not so sure.

For Meditation This Day
Let me not take the ground for granted, O God, neither in my treatment of it nor in my treatment of others upon it. The ground itself bears witness to my keeping—and grieving—of brother and sister.

Wednesday

Genesis 4:13-16 **Marked by Grace**

*And the Lord put a mark on Cain, so that
no one who came upon him would kill him.*

A "MARKED MAN." In our parlance, the phrase suggests one
targeted or consigned to some inevitable (and usually
negative) end. God marks Cain in a way the text does not
specify. However, the purpose of the marking is clear: Cain's
safety.

Cain's safety? The same Cain who murdered his brother in
cold blood, the same Cain whom God cursed to be a fugitive
and a wanderer—now protected by God's marking? Fortunately
the God of Genesis does not have to face the rigors of a polit-
ical campaign for reelection to divinity. This God is far too soft
on crime. First God defers the predetermined "immediate"
punishment of death for the disobedience of Cain's parents.
Now their murdering son receives sanctuary in his wanderings
east of Eden.

How would you describe God's marking of Cain: permis-
sive, inexplicable, indulgent...or gracious?

Genesis sometimes stretches the sensibilities in much the
same way the Gospels do in recounting Jesus' ministry. A
dying thief on a cross finds the promise of paradise, while an
admirable young man who kept all the laws from his youth
goes away sad. A woman receives commendation for an extrav-
agant outpouring of expensive oil that could have been sold to
care for the poor. Jesus shares table fellowship with tax collec-
tors and other assorted (and sordid) low-lifes. Why? The

answer, as with Cain, stems from grace: God's unconditional favor on those fashioned in God's image.

God marks Cain by grace. When life should have gone forfeit, God grants sanctuary. The reason surely does not reside in Cain: His plea with God contains no act of remorse, no confession of wrongdoing. The reason remains within the heart of God.

God marks us by grace. When our life should go forfeit, God offers us sanctuary. Now you may protest, "I am not Cain; I have not shed a sibling's blood." We distance ourselves from grace when we perceive that our need of grace is not as great as others'. But consider another troubling gospel passage: "You have heard that it was said to those of ancient times, 'You shall not murder'; and 'whoever murders shall be liable to judgment.' But I say to you that if you are angry with a brother or sister,…if you insult a brother or sister…if you say, 'You fool'" (Matt. 5:21-22).

Where do you fall on that spectrum? The need of grace does not confine itself to a grossly evil act, as with Cain. The need of grace also arises from the daily hardenings of heart to God and neighbor and one's own creation in the image of God. God's marking of our lives by grace is no less life-saving than God's marking of Cain—and as with Cain, God's reason for extending grace to us remains in the heart of God.

The rite of baptism carries something of that mystery, particularly when its waters mark the forehead of an infant. A cooing child makes no claim of merit established by dutiful churchgoing or self-giving service or doctrinally proper confession. Parents or sponsors may offer promises, but the waters spring from God's grace. That grace marked Cain with the promise of God's sanctuary, and that same grace marked us with God's image in our creation.

This first week of readings comes full circle to its beginning. God's fingerprints, evident in the dust of human creation, imprint Cain and us with the mark of God's grace. Seeds of blame and help, tragedy and hope, have been sown in the ground of human existence. The harvest remains to be seen.

For Meditation This Day
O God, touch me with your grace to forgive, to renew, to remind me of your image that I bear. Let me see and help me offer that same marking of grace upon all those I encounter.

～✑

Week Two

Matters of the Heart

Thursday

Genesis 6:1-5   **Hearts of Evil**

The Lord saw that the wickedness of humankind was
great...and that every inclination of the thoughts of
their hearts was only evil continually.

"T HE SHADOW," AN OLD RADIO MYSTERY SHOW, used to
preface each episode with the line: "Who knows what evil
lurks in the heart of men?" The implicit solution for each
subsequent mystery came in the accompanying refrain: "The
Shadow knows!" Though couched in melodrama, the show's
introduction touches on the theme that will weave through
this week's readings. Who knows the matters of the heart—
and what will be made of such knowledge?

The story of Noah frames this exploration. It is a *colorful*
story because of the rainbow and the animals. It is a *dreadful*
story because of the nearly universal destruction of life it
recounts. And, curiously, it is a *continuing* story because of
periodic attempts to recover the alleged remnants of the ark.

One rationale behind the recovery effort is the desire to
prove the text's truth. The difficulty with that desire lies in the
nature of the text's proclamation. The story of Noah stands
within the canon of scripture not primarily to recount a flood
or to provide a formula for shipbuilding. At its core, the story
of Noah reveals matters of the heart, both human and divine.

Discerning matters of the heart is no simple task. Think of
relationships you have had, times when you have wondered
"how it is" between you and another person. How have you
gauged what resides in another's heart? Words may reveal, but

words are subject to interpretation. Actions may show, but motives may remain hidden. Matters of the heart rely greatly on trust.

But trust, like hearts, can be broken. The first four verses of this day's reading recount tales that sound to us more like Greek mythology than Hebrew Scriptures: stories of "giants" (Nephilim) and the intermingling of "the daughters of humans" with "the sons of God" (6:4). The text's brevity is long on wonder and short on explanation. However, something seems out of place. The relationship between God and creation appears skewed by this obscuring of the boundaries. A crisis looms—a crisis of the heart. Wickedness (6:5) is the first name given to the condition that clogs the human heart. The connection between wickedness and the actions described in the preceding verses is unclear. But the consequences in the human heart are obvious: "Every inclination of the thoughts of their hearts was only evil continually."

One is tempted to relegate this judgment, which also speaks of giants and divine-human offspring, to the category of exaggeration. But evil remains potent in the human heart. In the inclinations of those who abduct and terrorize, of those who carry out ethnic cleansing, of those who see in skin color the excuse for hate and murder: The capacity of the heart for evil remains intact.

God is not oblivious to evil, for God knows the human heart—your heart. What will God see there? Hints of grace, glimpses of promise, resignations to that which cheapens life? Matters of faith remain matters of heart.

For Meditation This Day

Open the corners of my heart, O God. Forgive its lodging of evil; renew its dwelling of Spirit; restore its capacity for good.

Friday

Genesis 6:6-8   Heart of Grief

*The Lord was sorry that he had made humankind
on the earth, and it grieved [God] to [the] heart.*

GRIEVED...TO THE HEART." Did you know that the capacity to suffer sets apart the God of the Hebrews from the gods of their neighbors? The Greeks in particular developed extensive philosophical boundaries that defined the prerequisites of divinity. *Impassibility* was one qualification: the inability to suffer. God as the Unmoved Mover of all things represented this ideal of divinity removed from, and therefore untouched by, human life and history.

Genesis 6:6 describes a different God. Human evil grieves this God to the heart. Do you believe that? Do you believe that grief can pain the very heart of God? Some people stumble over the Noah story because of their difficulty in conceiving of a flood that covered the earth and reduced its human inhabitants to one extended family. Even that issue stands secondary to the incredible idea of a God who suffers on account of the ones fashioned in the divine image. The text declares that God is grieved to the heart.

Perhaps the story would be easier if it asked us to believe in an impassible God: a God who sits aloof in judgment, coldly lashing out at creation as an utterly corrupt failure. However, Genesis reveals not anger and rage but grief and sorrow. This scene speaks less of an irate judge than it does of a bereaved parent, pained by the actions of a beloved child. It points to the kind of hurt parents experience when children do not live up to their potential.

We may liken God's grief here to the unstated grief in Jesus' parable of the prodigal son (or loving father). Place yourself within the heart of that parent. The child demands inheritance *now*, a barely veiled declaration that you have not died soon enough. Then watch him walk away from family and identity and straight into a living hell, knowing you can do nothing to change what is in that child's heart. All you can feel is your own heartbreak.

That parable and Genesis 6:6 belie the theologies that depict God as incapable of suffering. Closeness and vulnerability, not remoteness and impassibility, distinguish the heart of this God. God's pain and grieving make the impending judgment of the Flood not an easy and unflinching act of retributive justice but a bereaved letting go of what has already died.

And who is to say but that the waters soon to buoy up the ark come salted with tears...tears of a God who has been grieved to the heart.

For Meditation This Day

Holy God, in what ways have I grieved you? Have I failed your high calling in my creation by falling prey to lower callings that pain you by bringing pain to others? How have I grieved you?

⤳

Saturday

Genesis 6:8, 22   **Grace and Response**

Noah found favor in the sight of the Lord....
He did all that God commanded him.

THOUGH GRIEVED AT HUMAN EVIL, God does not close God's heart to human potential. Grace opens the heart of God and makes an opening for human life. "Noah found favor in the sight of the Lord" (6:8). Older biblical translations render "found favor" as "found grace." Before waters rise in judgment, God's favor flows. Grace finds an individual named Noah.

Throughout the biblical witness, grace has a way of finding individuals, of favoring unexpected ones. A gift of God's favor later answers an elderly Hannah's prayer with a child (1 Samuel 1:18-20). The greeting of God's favor eventually perplexes a young girl named Mary with its mystery of holy conception (Luke 1:28, 35). But now, in the beginnings of Genesis, the word of God's favor graces an already ancient Noah with the promise of covenant (6:18). The pattern is set: God favors; life follows.

The pattern stamps our own spiritual journeys, although we may be unaware of it. Every breath we take, every experience of joy, every gift of love: All trace back to the inclination of God to grace our lives with creation's gifts. Think again about the assertion in verse 8: "Noah found favor in the sight of the Lord." Repeat that sentence aloud, substituting your name for that of Noah. If someone asked you to explain what you meant, what would you point to as evidence for such grace? "You find favor in the sight of the Lord." Do you believe that?

With the extension of God's grace comes the opportunity for human response. God leaves room for persons to accept or ignore God's grace. Noah remained free to believe himself a favored creation of God or to disregard such a gift. Perhaps even more critical to this story and our own, Noah remained free to believe himself favored of God, yet do nothing about it. This portion of the Noah story affirms such leeway by relating God's commanding, not God's building, of an ark. God leaves the work of construction to Noah.

Years ago, preacher Harry Emerson Fosdick railed against those who suffered from "a glut of unutilized grace." Worship, fellowship, nurture: Such experiences make it possible for a person to hear time and again the word of God's favor. The question is, What does one make of that favor? How will grace affect the course and conduct of your everyday life? More to the point, what does it mean for you this day to hear of God's favor for you?

Genesis depicts Noah as the recipient of God's grace. Yet hardly has God spoken this assurance than God gives the command to build. Grace bears a call to action. Again the biblical witness remains consistent. Mark's Gospel speaks of a man who approaches Jesus asking what must be done to inherit eternal life. The text says Jesus loved the man (Mark 10:21), surely an expression of favor. Yet, as with Noah, grace brings a call to action—a command to give.

In Mark's Gospel, the man walks away from giving; and in doing so, walks away from grace. Noah builds an ark; and in doing so, builds on grace. What of you? God in Christ speaks the word of favor to you—a favor whose belief awaits your action, a grace whose acceptance becomes incarnate in your response.

For Meditation This Day

Do I see myself as you see me, with eyes perceiving grace and favor? Do I act as one whose life is loved by the Creator of all? Help me see as you see. Help me act accordingly.

~

Sunday

Genesis 8:1-5   **Saving Remembrance**

*But God remembered Noah and all the wild animals
and all the domestic animals that were with him in the ark.*

"THE SEARCH FOR MIND" is the first of a nine-part documentary entitled *The Mind*. This first segment included an extraordinary testimony to the way our capacity to remember influences all of life. It featured a man named Clive whose entire faculty for memory had been lost due to a bout with viral encephalitis. As a result, he lived without memory—literally. The present was all he knew or recognized.

For example, the documentary showed a notebook he kept, its pages filled with line after line of entries like this: "11:54 A.M. I am now completely awake for the first time." The next line, whose recorded time differed only by a few minutes, attested to the same initial awakening to life and consciousness. While overjoyed by a visit from his wife, Clive told her this was the first time he had ever set eyes on her. No remembrance of their relationship or life together remained.

The most notable exception to this absence of memory came when his wife brought Clive to a church where he had regularly practiced with choristers. Clive had been an outstanding musician—singer, chorus master, conductor, and the world's leading expert on one of the Renaissance composers.

Somehow, as he sat at the piano with sheet music before him, his remembrance of music came alive. He caressed the keys in a sensitive accompaniment to a trio's anthem, skillfully conducting them and lending his own voice to the harmony. Once the piece ended, his body jerked uncontrollably for a few moments—and all was gone. No remembrance of the performance remained.

Consider how we take the power of memory for granted in our lives, as if those remembrances will always be there for us to summon at will: remembrances of cherished relationships, remembrances of special places, remembrances of who we are and how we have come to be that way. Memory possesses the power to give life by calling to mind and heart and spirit our experiences with others and with God.

Only with such valuing of remembrance can the "holy ground" of God's remembrance of Noah and the others be approached rightly. Genesis reveals God in this passage not only as the One who remembers but as the One whose remembrance brings life! God's remembrance becomes the means by which the ark comes to rest on solid ground. Things happen when this God remembers: Winds blow, waters subside, and a whole creation draws a deep breath of life from the One who is its source. Remembrance conveys grace.

The saving grace of remembrance need not always come packaged in the binding of nature's furies. The ability of remembrance to give life might await something as simple as a phone call to one long forgotten. To be remembered by another, in the midst of loneliness or depression, can buoy up life now as it did then. God gifts us with the ability to remember, a gift with which we may grace—and be graced by—the lives of others.

When all is said and done, God remains the One from whom remembrance comes as a life-saving grace. When the death of loved ones confronts us, we draw peace and comfort from our ability to remember experiences shared with those who no longer journey with us. Even more powerfully, we trust that God's remembrance will not allow those persons, among whom we will one day be numbered, to be lost. The hope of resurrection is a hope of God's remembering persons into new life…including Clive. Revelation 21:4 affirms that the only things forgotten will be death, pain, and tears. God will remember our lives. And in that saving remembrance, we will come to rest on the mount of God's grace, delivered to live for all time beyond time.

For Meditation This Day

Remember me, O God, when I feel alone and abandoned. Remember me when I feel lost. And may I remember you, who are always with me, who will always be with me, that I too may come to rest.

~

Monday

Genesis 8:6-12   **Waiting**

*[Noah] waited another seven days, and again he sent out the dove from the ark; and the dove came back.…
Then he waited another seven days.*

IF JOB IS THE CHARACTER FROM THE HEBREW Scriptures commended for patience, Noah might well be the one acclaimed for waiting. The waiting is explicit in today's reading as Noah waits to see whether the waters have subsided enough to disembark. But consider the waiting required of Noah throughout the story:

- waiting during the ark's construction, when the ridicule of neighbors perhaps was mingled with his own wonderings over whether God would indeed act;
- waiting during the rains, when the grief of creation's loss might have conspired with a concern over whether the waters would ever stop or if the ship would hold;
- waiting during the interim when rain ceased but floods remained, when the slowness of receding (the NRSV text says 150 days) must have seemed an eternity.

Noah waited—waited for the grief in God's heart to subside, and life to return. And we wait. To be sure, we wait for those things measured by calendars and clocks. As youth, we wait for the coming of adulthood's imagined freedoms. As workers, we wait for labor's time to end and leisure's to begin. But even more importantly, we wait for matters of the heart. We wait to find love and trust in our relationships—and then we wait to see if the relationships hold true.

Matters of the heart unfold slowly. Waiting is a requirement of faith, whether in another person or in God. Having faith implies that we will not coerce the other to act. Sometimes the act of love or grace does not come all at once, immediately, like a flash of light in a night sky. Sometimes it unfolds like a rose opening to the sun. Your eyes do not see the movement. But if you wait, the bud becomes a bloom.

Waiting on God's grace can be like that. Not because God is tardy and recalcitrant but simply because God's good grace does not always mesh lockstep with more rushed schedules. And so faith calls upon us to wait. To wait as did Noah. There is irony in Noah's waiting, you know. He sends the dove out a third time, not to bring back proof of its alighting on land—

but to find in its return the hope that the time is right. Noah's waiting finds fulfillment only by an act of faith. Any number of reasons might explain the dove's not returning: losing its way, falling prey to predator or sea. Yet Noah waits in hope that receives its unseen confirmation through the dove's absence.

What we wait for in life cannot always be seen from afar—particularly in matters of the heart, especially in matters of God's grace. We wait for what we trust will be revealed to us. The partner of such waiting is not uncontradicted proof but unswerving faith.

In waiting to see what becomes of a dove set loose, Noah waits to see what has become of God's heart. Will its favor bear him to dry land, fresh start, and new covenant? Lent provides a similar vigil for our waiting. We journey through Genesis; we journey toward Jerusalem; and we wait to see what will become of God's heart. We wait, trusting that God's hands still work in our lives. We wait, trusting that God's heart still holds us in favor and grace. We wait...trusting...God.

For Meditation This Day
In the midst of my service, teach me to wait: to wait in trust, to wait in hope, to wait upon the inclination of your heart.

~

Tuesday

Genesis 8:20-22   **As Much As Things Change**

"The inclination of the human heart is evil from youth."

CLEAN SLATES. FRESH STARTS. Have you ever found your-self yearning for such new beginnings in your life? Sometimes the longing evolves from heights of joy and blessing. Before an altar, a couple speaks words of commitment and trust, giving life to the new covenant between them. They stand free to fashion and form their relationship from that moment on as they choose.

Sometimes the longing struggles to emerge from tragedy and remorse. In the aftermath of mistakes, great and small, we wish for the possibility to start over again, to undo regretted wrongs and to redo neglected rights. We might even find ourselves vowing to be new persons if given that second chance.

At the heart of this story is God's intent to give creation a clean slate, a fresh start. The one favored to carry the hopes of that new beginning was righteous and blameless Noah. Noah confirms the merit of God's choice by his first act off the ark: the offering of sacrifice to God.

Now had the Noah story ended with this offering, creation's future needs for renewal might have been fulfilled by periodic catastrophes that left the guileless untouched and the guilty unmourned. But notice the astonishing word slipped into God's vow never again to destroy creation: "for the inclination of the human heart is evil from youth." Righteous Noah, blameless Noah, Noah buoyed up by the ark to find deliverance for self and family and the animals—the heart of Noah shows the trace of evil. Even the best and brightest bears this cardiac infirmity.

But the truly remarkable element in this assessment traces back to God's previous assessment and plan of action in chapter 5. There, the inclination of the human heart toward evil results in God's judgment. In chapter 8, that same inclination results in the promise of God's grace: "Never again!"

And therein lies the curious yet powerful thrust of this story. Namely, that as far as human beings go, as much as things change; things stay the same. Forty days of rain and ensuing months of flood do not change the human heart. But incredibly, they do change the heart of God from judgment to grace, from sorrow over creation to its sworn preservation: "Never again!"

Can you believe that? Can you believe a God who sees the human heart as it truly is and still chooses grace? The text asks us to affirm an extraordinary thing—and not just about how it was with old Noah. The God who sees the human heart as it truly is and still chooses grace, is the God who rummages around in our lives and hearts and sees us as we are.

For those of us who'd rather not admit to things like failings and evil as part of our identity, the story is discomforting. For those of us who'd rather have God repeat the onslaught of Genesis 6 on sin and evil, the story is unsatisfying. But for those of us who long for fresh starts and clean slates, the story is gospel. It promises the hope of renewal, the hope of God's taking us as we are and still managing to fashion the work of new creation through us. In the final analysis, grace arises not out of who we are but out of who God chooses to be. Thanks be to God!

For Meditation This Day
Teach me, O God, to see the grace you hold me in; that I, in turn, might seek the change that grace would bring.

Genesis 9:8-17   **Covenant**

*"As for me, I am establishing my covenant with you
and your descendants after you, and with every
living creature that is with you."*

T O THOSE ONCE CRADLED IN THE ARK, God declares a new
word: *covenant*. In the ancient Near East, covenant did not
necessarily mean an equality of standing between the partners. Covenant did, however, mean a yoked and committed
relationship.

The Mosaic covenant often dominates our understanding
of covenant. It narrates a relationship where law figures largely,
where caricatures of legalism strip this covenant of its fundamentally gracious character. Yet, according to Genesis, God
struck a gracious covenant prior to Sinai, a covenant clearly
visible and broadly inclusive.

"As for me…," it begins. The covenant does not issue from
Noah's hard-fought negotiation or overdue recognition. Covenant issues from the heart of God, and its blessing comes unbid-
den save for God's intent: "I am establishing my covenant."

"With you and your descendants." The gracious nature of
God's covenant making unfolds in its falling upon generations
unborn, persons whose choices have not yet revealed what sort
of partners they will make. Even the inclusion of Noah under-
scores covenant's dependence on grace. God's declaration that
ark-borne hearts still carry the inclination of evil (8:21) does
not exempt Noah from that assessment. Yet neither does that
assessment exempt Noah from the gift of covenant.

Had God concluded the covenant community at this point we would marvel at the wideness of God's mercy. But now the circle expands to include "every living creature that is with you" (9:10). The grace revealed in life's creation extends itself to the breadth of those incorporated in God's covenant. Turkey and zebra, ocelot and aardvark, platypus and marmoset: The list is enough to make one smile, if not guffaw. And as if to make sure we understand who the covenant partners are, this passage connects covenant with "every living creature" or "all flesh" four more times.

Now I admit that this vision of God's covenant community is bewildering. What's the point of including animals? Any number of species—especially those species that human ignorance has brought to extinction—might counter with, "What's the point of including humans?" But perhaps both questions are the right ones. The purpose of God's including animals is the purpose behind God's including humans: grace. The ability to think or reason is not the determining qualification for inclusion in this covenant nor is the possession of spirit that may (or may not) distinguish one species from another. God's community takes shape on God's terms. And those terms are grace.

The Noah covenant stretches the imagination. Whenever we stand ready to narrow the circle of God's community or to act in disregard of those whom we define as outside the circle, this covenant, by the very breadth of its grace, should give us pause. Somehow the grace of God has seen fit to enter into covenant with people like me, with people like you, with people unlike either one of us—and with every living creature.

Perhaps that is why this covenant takes the rainbow as its sign. Long before words graven on stone or cups shared in remembrance involved reason to perceive the meaning of covenant, all of God's creatures could see a bow in the sky. A bow promised sun's hope in the midst of rain's fall—life's hope from the hand of covenant's maker.

For Meditation This Day

Remind me of all those with whom I share your covenant; help me treat them as those you have chosen in grace, just as you have chosen me.

⁓

Week Three

Journeys

Thursday

Genesis 11:1-9   Scattered by God

From [Babel] the Lord scattered them
abroad over the face of all the earth.

BABEL. THE VERY SOUND OF the ancient city's name mimics the confusion that descended upon its inhabitants. The text itself makes that connection in verse 9, linking the name of Babel with the Hebrew word *balal*, meaning "to confuse." Another ancestor of Babel's name points to the story's crisis: the Semitic *babilu*, "gate of God."

To the tower-builders on the plain of Shinar, the "gate of God" loomed within the reach of careful planning and diligent effort. Their pathway to heaven consisted of brick and bitumen. As you listen to the text, the gate of God rises not so much in search of deity as in assertion of human identity and place: "Let us make a name for ourselves; otherwise we shall be scattered abroad upon the face of the whole earth." In other words, "Here we stand."

Genesis 10 narrates the fulfillment of God's command to fill the earth, as Noah's descendants "spread abroad on the earth." It is interesting to consider how this spreading devolved from divine mandate to human fear. Perhaps the travelers had had enough of movement and change. The Babel version of digging in one's heels to stay put entails the residents' digging in their tower—their gate of God. The name of Babel offers no clue as to whether the building of this gate had to do with forging access to God or limiting God's approach to them. After all, gates can be drawn shut and locked.

Name-making and tower-building do not cease with the

descent of babble on Babel, by any means. Nationalism and racism arise from the desire to elevate one's own name or cause above all others. Too much attention to "making a name for ourselves" dulls the valuing of those who bear other names. Too much attention to "building ourselves a city" neglects the work God intends for the benefit of others and earth's restoration.

And so judgment falls. Only now the torrents are not of waters but languages. A flood of tongues spills across Shinar's plain, scattering its inhabitants over the face of the earth.

Scattering. Its judgment is what the people of Shinar feared all along. And yet its grace is what God intended all along. Scattering: to fill the earth, to spread abroad the nations.

Therein lies the irony of Babel. The grace of God, extended to restore human life across the earth, is feared. The resistance to living by God's providential purposes takes form in seizing control, making a name, erecting a monument to autonomy. But grace proves irresistible, even if it comes veiled in judgment.

Even now grace retains an element of fear. We experience the fear of grace when we do not understand its purposes, when arrogance takes primacy in life. In those contexts, God's grace may indeed create dread of judgment—judgment that would shake us free from self-absorption, judgment that would topple our alluring towers of self-importance to remind us of God's sovereignty. Then once again we might experience the grace of relationship with God and neighbor.

Many link the Babel text to that of Pentecost, when the confusion of languages finds at least momentary resolution. Yet consider what Pentecost inaugurates: the scattering of the gospel, and eventually the apostles, across the earth. God continues to scatter us, as with the people on Shinar's plain, uprooting us from the comfortable and familiar for the sake of earth's restoration. As those fashioned in God's image, our scattering intends to bring that image to places and persons in need of grace's restoration, in need of a glimpse into God's redemptive purposes.

For those wishing to live in isolation, scattering levies God's judgment. For those choosing to live in faith, scattering unleashes God's grace. How is it for you?

For Meditation This Day
Holy God, keep my rooting in faith from becoming root-bound.

～

Friday

Genesis 12:1-5   **Trust Walk**

So Abram went, as the Lord had told him.

A SEMINARY PROFESSOR TOLD OF THE TIME he played the dual role of father-of-the-bride and presiding minister at his daughter's wedding. All things proceeded routinely until the exchange of the vows.

When the groom concluded his promise of fidelity, the professor turned to his daughter and asked, "Do you believe what he just said?" He went on to ask the same question of the groom after his daughter's vow. During the homily, the minister/father spoke of the role that belief and trust play in empowering marriage's promises. The fulfillment of such promises requires not only sincerity from the one who offers them but trust from his or her recipient. Why? Without trust, promises are not engaged. Without trust, they likely will not be reciprocated. Covenant, marital and other, depends on the trusting of promises.

The relationship between promise and trust looms large in the stories of Abram/Abraham. Nowhere is this more true than in God's initial call to Abram: "Go from your country...to the land that I will show you." Abram's affirmative response would involve leaving home and kin, setting aside a familiar and secure life in order to set out on a road not yet traveled. Promises served as Abram's primary companions at the outset of his journey. Promises of land without an accompanying deed, promises of being a blessing to the nations without certainty of his own family's well-being, promises of an heir without benefit of an ultrasound to confirm the diagnosis.

The familiarity of Abram's call may cloak the barriers to the trust required of him—and through him, of us. Who among us would leave all that is familiar if the call comes in the disorienting time following a parent's death? Who among us would plod diligently ahead if the destination reveals a land already populated and claimed as home by others? Who among us would continue to trust in an identity of being a "blessing to the nations" when time and again new neighbors bring new conflicts?

God does not ask Abram to adhere to a series of theological propositions about the nature of deity. God asks Abram to go: to literally set one foot after the other on a path that leads him further and further from what he can take for granted, further and further into the realm of what he must trust. Grace bears extraordinary promise. The catch, both then and now, is the greater the promise, the greater the trust.

Abram heard. Abram trusted. Abram walked.

In scripture and community, through worship and spiritual discipline, God offers us the same promise of gracious relationship. Do we hear God's call in that promise, offering new life and fresh grace? In Jesus Christ, you and I receive the pledge of God's own self to us. The question once asked of a daughter and son-in-law becomes ours as well: Do you believe what (and whom) God promises? If we so trust, then we should so walk. "So Abram went."

For Meditation This Day

Holy One, you promise more than can be imagined. Grant me trust enough to follow, even when your promises go beyond my sight.

~

Saturday

Genesis 16:1-11   **Taking Matters into Our Hands**

"You have given me no offspring" (Gen. 15:3).

I T IS ONE THING TO SAY WE WILL ROOT our lives in the trusting of promises when all falls smoothly and swiftly into place. It is quite another to maintain trust in those promises when time delays or experience deters their fulfillment. Promises birthed of God's grace come without timetable—and promises deferred test the limits of our trust. In such circumstances, conventional wisdom suggests that we attain our heart's desires not by faith and waiting but by our own skill and cunning.

Ten years after arriving in Canaan, the land of promise, Abram and Sarai remain childless. Without an heir, land holds no more promise than to serve as Abram and Sarai's burial ground. Without an heir to till and hold, land and promise lie fallow.

Rather than continuing to wait upon the reliability of the promise and the Promise-Giver, the recipients of the promise choose to take fulfillment into their own hands. They exchange the mysteries of God for the vulgarities of human pragmatism: "Go in to my slave-girl; it may be that I shall obtain children by her." Abram follows Sarai's words. Hagar becomes pregnant.

As the story unfolds, the frailty of attempting to fulfill God's promises by taking matters into one's own hands becomes painfully clear. Autonomous initiative has a way of outstripping foresight. Neither Abram nor Sarai expect Hagar's ensuing contempt. The gracious promise of an heir twists into the jealous threat of a rival. The failure of trust eventuates in the harsh judgment of banishment upon a woman who has been used and now discarded, upon an unborn child who stirs blameless in the womb.

The crisis generated in this narrative is not primarily one of morality but of trust. Abram's (and Sarai's) basic error occurs not in engaging or suggesting sexual relations outside the bond of marriage. Rather, Abram and Sarai sell out the uncertainty and faith-dependent nature of the promise for instant fulfillment. Abram chooses not to wait on the promise but to rely on his own prowess. When matters turn out differently than expected, Sarai chooses to exercise not grace but judgment.

The ungracious action of Abram and Sarai toward Hagar, however, finds counterpoint in God's unyielding commitment to grace. The commitment first delivers Hagar—the rejected one, the banished one, the one who played no previous role in the covenant promises. This one is now the blessed of God, as is her son Ishmael, and as will be her countless descendants. Ishmael, Hebrew for "the God who sees," serves as an incarnate reminder that grace does not overlook the outsider.

Though it goes beyond the scope of this text, God's commitment to grace also delivers Abram and Sarai—the proud ones, the judging ones, the ones who abdicated their trust in the promises of covenant. These same ones remain the blessed of God, as will be their son, as will be their countless descendants.

That God's grace encompasses all these persons offers hope to us. Like Hagar, we may feel swept up by the actions of those holding power over us or simply be caught up in circumstances beyond our control. Yet we are not forgotten or overlooked. God sees our situation, and God acts with grace. Like Abram and Sarai, we likely have our times of putting trust aside in order to solve matters all on our own—only to discover our frightful ineptitude at manipulating things for the good. Yet God does not discard us, replacing us with those of perfect trust. God remembers the promise, and God seeks us with grace. A seeking that calls us back to trust, to patience, to the One who fulfills the promises of grace in God's good time and in God's good way.

For Meditation This Day
God, when I'm tempted to take matters into my hands, remind me of the strength and wisdom of your hands. Then may I act with trust.

Sunday

Genesis 17:1-16   **What's in a Name?**

*"No longer shall your name be Abram, but your name
shall be Abraham. . . . you shall not call her Sarai,
but Sarah shall be her name."*

HOW MANY TIMES DOES AN INFANT hear his or her name spoken before linking that sound with his or her being? How many times did you hear your name vocalized before eyes brightened and lips turned upward and throat cooed in recognition?

That process leading to self-recognition remains a mystery. It has to do with repetition of the sound, to be sure. An infant who rarely hears his or her name spoken may not have adequate opportunity to make the connection between those bits of phonetic percussion vibrating on developing eardrums and a dawning sense of self. One wonders, *If the repetition of the name rumbles only in harsh or angry tones, will an infant want to be known by that sound?* Will that name become more of a burden than a blessing? If a name brings blessing, grace will have played a part. Blessing will have come in the grace of a parent or caregiver's speaking that name with love and enacting that love in deed.

Take the story of Abram/Abraham and Sarai/Sarah. These two are no mere children, by any means. Abram stands at the brink of ninety-nine years of age, while Sarai can claim only a decade less. They have carried their names through all these years. Names, like identities, become habit over such a length of time. And once identity becomes routine and entrenched, what one has been tends to determine what one will become.

That is why bestowing new names upon Abram (Abraham) and Sarai (Sarah) represents a gracious act of God's covenant-renewal with them—and its possibilities with us. God's naming of these two testifies to this nearly century-old couple that their lives still cradle new promise. Abram "the exalted ancestor" becomes Abraham "the father of multitudes." Sarai, still barren, receives the christening of Sarah: "princess." What (and who) they have been does not limit their potential. New names promise new birth, literally and figuratively.

Do you need a new name? Few persons would identify that as a pressing need. But do you need new birth, new hope, new promise in your life? That is where this story speaks with greatest power. One does not need to attain the age of ninety-nine to experience the "slipping away" of long-sought dreams or to realize that life seems to have passed you by. One does not need to go childless to feel loneliness or lack of fulfillment with what one has done thus far with the gift of years. Middle age can bring such reflection when we assess our lack of accomplishment to this point. Even youth, staring at choices of vocation and relationship, may wonder if life is already laid out and decided.

"No longer shall your name be...." Names and identities can change. God's grace has a way of opening new doors, of unleashing new thoughts, of making possible new lives. Like an infant learning to recognize her name, we find it may take us awhile to recognize the possibilities with which God's grace christens us. For most, recognition involves the repetition of such grace: spoken through the stories of scripture, enacted through the support of community, experienced through the moving of Spirit.

Such grace made it possible for Abram to become Abraham, for Sarai to become Sarah. Who will grace enable you to become?

For Meditation This Day

For knowing me by name, O God, I give you thanks; for helping me know who I may yet become, O God, I pray your guidance.

~

Monday

Genesis 17:17-18, 18:1-15   **Laughter**

Then Abraham fell on his face and laughed (17:17).
So Sarah laughed to herself (18:12).

PICTURE THIS SCENE: THE ANCIENT PATRIARCH Abraham rolls on the ground, doubled over from stifling a guffaw. He finally blurts out something to God about Ishmael's still being a viable option for covenanthood.

And picture this one: The ancient matriarch Sarah darts back behind the tent's flap so as not to tip off her barely concealed laughter, questioning how a couple so past their prime could have the pleasure required in the creating of a child. When God asks Abraham what made his wife snicker, she backpedals in a flight of denial that would make a caught-with-his-hand-in-the-cookie-jar politician green with spin-control envy.

In both instances, God promises the seemingly impossible gift of an heir. In both instances, Abraham and Sarah laugh. Why? Maybe the fairer question is, Why not? Why not laugh in the face of incredulity?

We laugh when cartoons depict gravity's pull on one character who runs off the edge of a cliff but not another. We laugh when comedians narrate childhood football games where the winning pass route involves catching a bus and then a subway in order to intersect with a pigskin whose hang-time is measured not in seconds but minutes. Something in us makes us disposed to laughter when the limits of reality stretch beyond the ordinary bounds of sense and reason.

And isn't that exactly what grace does: stretch the limits of reality beyond the ordinary bounds? Isn't that what a promise of a child is to a couple who might well be on the downside of their diamond anniversary?

So for starters, let's not begrudge Abraham and Sarah their laughter. The fact that they laugh makes them human. And perhaps even more significantly, their laughter indicates their realization that something extraordinary is on the loose, something so otherwise incredulous that laughter is the best—even the most faithful—thing they can do at the moment.

Grace can do that to a person. The moment you learn of a pregnancy or birth, the instant you hear of a kin's or friend's safety after involvement in some jeopardy, the twinkling when you discover love for another or find yourself loved: In such times, laughter is the most appropriate response—or tears. Then again, it is hard to separate the two. They often flow together.

God promised grace; Abraham and Sarah laughed. Maybe you can remember when grace has so moved you that you couldn't hold in a smile or resist an ironic chuckle or let loose with a belly laugh—or maybe you can't. We religious folk have become masters at clinging to the serious nature of theology and faith. But at what cost? Jesus once castigated those who mistakenly equated looking dismal with being pious. (See Matt. 6:16.)

God promised grace; Abraham and Sarah laughed. God did not censure their reaction. Even the question of "Why?" asked about Sarah resulted in no reprimand. Fear resulted in her denial of laughter. Fear may do the same with us—crippling our emotions, keeping us from experiencing the fullness of joy God means to bring to us. Laughter belongs to celebration, and grace deserves celebration: the celebration of an aged couple for a child still-promised, the celebration of a parent for a child once-prodigal. The stories may differ, but the point is always the same. Faith calls us to celebrate God's reality-changing and limit-breaking grace.

Abraham and Sarah never did get over the laughter. At the birth of the promised child, they named him "Laughter" (the meaning of Isaac in Hebrew). The child of grace. The child of laughter. May we laugh and learn.

For Meditation This Day

O God, help me find joy in your grace and free me to express that joy. For you are the God of Abraham and Sarah—and Laughter.

~~~

Tuesday

Genesis 18:16-33   **For the Sake of...**

"Will you indeed sweep away the righteous with the wicked?"

IN THE STEPHEN VINCENT BENÉT SHORT STORY "The Devil and Daniel Webster," the famous orator and lawyer of nineteenth-century New England defends a farmer from a pact entered into with "Old Scratch." In spite of the signed document and a jury selected from hell's most infamous inmates, Webster wins the case and his client goes free.

If the premise and outcome of that story strike you as too incredible, then good luck with this day's tale of Abraham's bartering with God over the fate of Sodom and Gomorrah. The scene calls to mind the haggling one might encounter over a merchant's table in a Middle Eastern market. Abraham argues the price from a starting point of fifty down to ten. But in this haggling, the merchandise is the welfare of the city, and the cost is the number of righteous within it.

Several things make this story riveting. First is the status given to Abraham. The early verses relate God's choice to disclose the situation regarding Sodom and Gomorrah to Abraham. Why? So Abraham will be a force for righteousness and justice among those under his charge and so God's promises may come to pass. In other words, God acknowledges the responsibility entrusted to Abraham for what will come of this covenant. A variant in the text of verse 22 even leaves it unclear as to whether Abraham stands before God or God stands before Abraham. Either way, God allows Abraham to serve as a forceful and persuasive advocate for the sake of others.

That advocacy moves the narrative to an even more startling revelation: the influence of the righteous among the guilty. Conventional wisdom declares that one bad apple can spoil the whole barrel. Abraham's plea and God's adopted vulnerability to it move in the opposite direction. "Suppose there are fifty righteous within the city;...suppose five of the fifty are lacking?...Suppose forty are found there....thirty.... twenty....ten...." At every step, Abraham presses God to show grace. Notice too that the plea is not on behalf of the fifty or the forty or the ten. For the sake of however few righteous, Abraham argues, "Will you destroy the whole city?" Abraham actually serves as an advocate for the fate of the unrighteous majority.

How do you and I measure up in that arena? It is not too difficult to rise up in protest when the innocent suffer, and the good are trampled upon. But Abraham far exceeds that here. He appeals and cajoles God with gritty persistence for grace to fall on the heads of those who have become a byword for human sin. Do we so earnestly seek the welfare of the ones whose choices, lifestyles, and reputations define iniquity in our day? Or are we more inclined to nod our heads and bite our lips in solemn virtuosity when bad things happen to obviously bad people?

For the sake of Sodom and Gomorrah, no less, Abraham stood before God. Why? Maybe Abraham remembered God's first calling to him, where mission linked the command to "go" with the promise that "in you, all the families of the earth shall be blessed" (12:3). All the families. Not just the ones that say their prayers every night, not just the ones that teach their children well, not just the ones that are paragons of morality. No, all the families shall be blessed. And as Abraham knew through experience and trust, blessing involved grace. So for the sake of families with whom his own righteousness stood in sharp contrast, Abraham pleaded.

For whom do we plead? For whose sake do we appeal and cajole God with gritty persistence for grace to fall? May Abraham teach us the breadth of families for whom we may yet be a blessing.

For Meditation This Day
Teach me humility of heart and expanse of concern, holy God, so my life may serve as blessing—not bane—for others.

~

Wednesday

Genesis 21:1-7 — A Child Is Born

Sarah conceived and bore Abraham a son.

THE JOURNEY TO A PROMISED LAND now finds parallel in this journey to a promised child. It can be a long road between conception and birth, in some ways far longer than the road that led from Haran to Canaan. Hope and nausea, unbearable pain and exquisite joy: Childbearing and childbirth blend such experiences until they are inseparable. So a lifetime stretches out unspoken between the lines of "Sarah conceived and bore a son."

Grace can involve such waiting and nurturing among us. What seems like a lifetime may pass from the time we sense its first stirrings within until its life surges through and out of us in newborn faith. We need to discover as true the inklings of God's love and acceptance for us before we trust such love and acceptance with our lives. However, unlike childbearing, gracebearing does not have a relatively set length of time from conception to birth. What seems like a lifetime can actually be a lifetime. But when birth does comes, of child or grace, the joy overwhelms the wait.

While birth in this story brings fulfillment to promises spoken from of old, birth also engenders new promises that await fruition. The arrival of the longed-for child gives rise to a new set of expectations and dreams—expectations for how life will be with this Isaac, dreams for how this fragile bundle of tissue and nerve and spirit will embody the covenant's next generation. Fulfillment yields to fresh hope in God's purposes; birth issues in new conceptions of God's grace.

A child is born. Hope rarely finds clearer expression among us. At birth, all is possibility, an open book waiting to be written. Little wonder that centuries later Isaiah would choose the image of a child's birth to awaken hope in the possibilities of God's messianic rule: "For a child has been born for us." Or that Jesus, in prefacing his disclosure of "God so loved the world," would baffle a learned Pharisee with the need to be born again: born like a child, for whom all is potential by the grace of God.

By the grace of God, we are born. Anyone reading these words has already experienced that gift of birth. By the grace of God, we may yet be born. Anyone reading these words still has the potential for that gift of new birth. Grace's conception is never a once-and-for-all event to which we may never return. Every time the Spirit stirs our hearts to fresh compassion, every time God's creative power reshapes our wills to faithful obedience, every time Christ's presence rejuvenates our service or devotion, new life stirs within us; and we journey toward rebirth. A journey whose promise is this: A child is born...the child of God whom grace fashioned you and me to be.

For Meditation This Day
Made in your image, may my spirit conceive and my life deliver the grace that is mine in Christ Jesus.

～୨

Week Four

~⌒

The Eye of the Storm

Thursday

Genesis 22:1-8   **Through the Eyes of a Child**

*Isaac said to his father Abraham, "Father!...
The fire and the wood are here, but where is the lamb?"*

I N HIS BOOK *FEAR AND TREMBLING*, the Danish theologian
Søren Kierkegaard made the following observation on this
narrative: "The ethical expression for what Abraham did is,
that he would murder Isaac; the religious expression is, that he
would sacrifice Isaac."

If you have any questions about the fairness or validity of
that ethical interpretation, all you need do is put this story into
the context of your own neighborhood and its children. A
father takes his child up a hillside out of town and there draws
a knife or gun by which he will end the child's life. If at that
moment you should stumble upon the scene and demand to
know why he plans to do this, he pleads obedience to a command from God.

What is your response? Do you laud him as saint for his
extraordinary faithfulness—or judge him as demonic for his
willingness to strip the innocent of life in the name of God? Do
you feel compelled to seek relationship with a God who engenders such absolute devotion, or do you flee as far and fast as you
can from a deity who commands the taking of a child's life?

The narrative of the journey to Mount Moriah is a myste-
rious one—wild and unkempt, yet an uneasy plodding of one
foot after the other as the offering at journey's end draws ever
closer. Unless one leaps to story's end, grace is a hard com-
modity to come by. And leaping to the end does no justice to
the way traveled by Abraham and by Isaac.

Isaac. Isaac is the forgotten character in this narrative. Traditional attention focuses almost exclusively on Abraham, the actor on the stage of faith's most trying test. But what of Isaac? What of the one who is to be acted upon in faith's name? To locate grace in this narrative, we must find it in—which is to say, find it for—Isaac. Grace cannot afford to disregard innocence, for innocence relies on grace for safekeeping.

"Father!" Isaac's first word affirms the tie of kinship. The text infers Isaac knows nothing of the test that initiated this journey. Isaac knows only the parent who walks beside him: a knowledge that begets trust, a trust that assumes safekeeping.

That assumption prevents Isaac from discerning the true significance of a missing lamb. Isaac asks where the lamb is with no hint of fear in the question. Abraham's ensuing reply that "God . . . will provide" seemingly does not arouse Isaac's anxiety. Why? Apparently, Isaac trusts. But does Isaac trust God's providence or Abraham's word? For a child, that may be a difficult distinction. Psychologists tell us that children form their first impressions of God from parents. A child's innocence and faith rely on the nurture of trusted ones. Whether those so trusted prove worthy, prove gracious is another matter. Here, that very matter sets Abraham and Isaac upon a journey.

Through the eyes of a child, the trek up the mountain called Moriah begins with trust. An innocent child relies on the gracious keeping of a parent. Isaac's trust in Abraham—and God—will find either its justification or undoing on Moriah.

For Meditation This Day

Do I really trust in you, O God? And do those who trust in me find nurture or jeopardy? Help me on my journey.

Friday

Genesis 22:9-14 **Through the Eyes of a Child**

So Abraham called that place "The Lord will provide."

YOUTHFUL EYES THAT ONCE STRAINED TO SEE Moriah's mount in the distance now take in other sights. They watch a father build an altar, perhaps uncertain why the elder's hands shake as they pile stone upon stone. They watch a father spread the wood across the altar, wood that Isaac himself had borne up this long hill for the still-to-be found lamb for the sacrifice.

And then, Isaac both sees and feels the remaining preparations. He sees the cords taken by Abraham, then feels them looped tightly around wrists and arms, ankles and legs. He feels his father take him in his arms, as Abraham had carried Isaac countless times before: in from the fields after play, off to bed after supper. Now, however, Isaac feels no lamb's wool blanket to cushion his rest but the jagged ends of dry branches poking into his back. At the last, a child's eyes watch as a knife is unsheathed, then poised above to strike. For Isaac, the trusting of Abraham's word that God would provide a lamb for this offering must have seemed a dream at best—a lie at worst.

Grace takes Isaac to the edge of life. Unlike those of us who read this story with outcome clearly in sight, Isaac awaits grace's providence all the way to the point of his father's drawn blade. When deliverance comes in a last-second intervention of God's voice and an entangled ram, I daresay we cannot imagine Isaac's relief. Not unless we have stood at that same precipice between life and death, with one foot dangling over and the other losing its balance. Not unless we have had our dearest trust tested to its absolute maximum.

Grace for Isaac is nothing to be presumed upon nor taken lightly. His child's eyes watch as, step by step, his hope becomes ever more distant. Only at the end does grace hold firm. As indicated in Abraham's naming of this place, God provided—a providing whose coming must have seemed awefully long to Isaac.

It is in such delay that this text, through Isaac's eyes, speaks of grace with greatest eloquence. When we experience God's providence immediately addressing our needs, God's grace needs no advocate or apologist. In those times, grace does not even require trust.

But Isaac's eyes bear witness to the all-too-familiar delay of grace. Isaac's eyes take in the same sights seen by a cancer patient, whose treatments exact a precious toll on body and spirit without providing definitive sign of healing. Isaac's eyes take in the same sights seen by innocents caught in any one of this world's crossfires: where life's routines go on in lethal circumstances, where cries of "how long?" go unanswered for too long. Isaac's eyes see the testimony that we do not yet live in the sovereign realm of God. Isaac's eyes see grace delayed—yet they also witness the coming of grace. Just when it seems time and hope have finally vanished, grace appears. The Lord does provide.

The eyes of Isaac bear witness to what is for many persons an agonizing time: the wait for grace to show its face, to deliver innocence, to restore life. On Mount Moriah, those who wait discern that God's grace will come, though not always as swiftly as they might wish.

But what of those for whom last-minute deliverance does

not come? Does God's grace ultimately abandon? For them, for all, another child would trudge up a mount—a child, like Isaac, weighed down by a load of wood for another sacrifice. A child in whom it would be said, God had provided the Lamb!

For Meditation This Day

God of Isaac, help me see your grace. When its coming is deferred, when its certainty is concealed, help me see through the eyes of a child, your child.

~

Saturday

Genesis 24:1-9   **On Not Going Back**

"See to it that you do not take my son back there."

AN OLD ADAGE STATES, "You can never go home again" Implied in those words is the understanding that one can never experience places (and persons) belonging to one's memory as they once were. Time brings change. People change.

This day's text begins with Abraham's directing his servant to find a wife for Isaac. The directive comes in the wake of Sarah's death, not long after her grieved husband finished piling the burial stones upon her body in the cave of the field of Machpelah in Canaan. Perhaps Abraham saw his own days numbered when he looked into Sarah's face one last time. Looking into her face, he also might have seen Isaac—Isaac, the promised child, still without wife or heir.

So mourning gives way to preparation in order that the promise may find an heir in another generation. "Go to my country and to my kindred and get a wife for my son Isaac" (24:4). Abraham imposes conditions on the search: The wife shall come from Abraham's own people rather than from the Canaanites. It is hard to say whether this owes more to the ethic of kinship marriage or the Israelites' aversion to all things Canaanite. When the servant raises the real concern that the woman might not return for a groom sight-unseen, Abraham commands the second condition—not once (24:6) but twice (24:8). Isaac may not return to his father's homeland. The solemnity of the search finds vivid depiction in the graphic concluding gesture of oath-taking (24:9).

"You must not take my son back there" (24:8). The urgency of Abraham's words are clear but what of the reasoning? Why not allow Isaac to travel to his father's home? For some, this text's opening verse suggests that one cannot return home because things are never as they once were—or imagined to be.

In the case of Isaac, another reason weighs against the return: his own identity as the child of promise. The promises that beckoned Abraham from the comfort—and prosperity—of home involved land and descendants. To date, all he had to show for land ownership was Sarah's burial plot. Fulfillment promised more than this humble beginning, but such fulfillment clearly stretched beyond Abraham's years. A wife's death likely convinced him of that. Now only a son's life remained.

So Isaac was the inheritor of promises still pending. But how could Isaac inherit the future if he returned to the past? The journey that Abraham undertook years before in search of the promises did not lead backward to Haran but forward into Canaan: "Go from your country and your kindred and your father's house to the land that I will show you" (12:1). The words that made it impossible for Abraham to return now do the same for Isaac.

God's promises present the same claim upon our lives and upon our faith. Each generation's inheritance of those promises occurs on journeys into the future, not on retreats into the past. We may find identity and kinship in what lies behind, but we encounter the living God on the way ahead.

Abraham made his servant swear that Isaac would never be taken "back there." Where is "back there"? The specifics vary from person to person. It depends on where one hears the siren song that concedes the struggle for what could be in resignation to what has been. Anywhere promises can be disregarded. Anywhere faith's journey might be becalmed. Those who live by gracious promises cannot go "back there." Not Isaac. Not you. Not me.

For Meditation This Day
God, what in my life, what in my longings puts your promises at risk? Show me the way forward; show me the way promised.

~

Sunday

Genesis 24:10-67   **The Respite of Love**

[Isaac] took Rebekah, and she became his wife;
and he loved her.

TESTING AND CONFLICT DOMINATE the stories of Isaac. Early on, those stories focus on a child nearly sacrificed by his own father. Later those stories reveal a family divided by deceit and jealousy. But in today's narrative, Isaac finds respite from all that troubled him before and all that would follow after. That respite comes in the person and love of Rebekah.

Genesis 24 recounts the story of how Abraham's servant came to find a wife for Isaac. Two things stand out in the account: First is the trust in God's providence to sustain the covenant. Twice the servant called on God to reveal "steadfast love" (*hesed*) for Abraham by revealing the one God had "appointed" for Isaac (24:14, 44). *Hesed* is a key word in Israel's covenant tradition. It describes the loyalty that binds partners and makes relationship trustworthy. Thus the servant admits that his mission hinges not on his own keen eye for a suitable wife but on God's *hesed*. That reliance on providence further elicits the servant's belief that a woman would be "appointed" for Isaac.

A second critical component of this account is the action by which the servant will recognize the "appointed": hospitality. Not only will she be the one who shows kindness to a stranger by offering water, she will be the one who gives drink to the stranger's animals. In the culture of the ancient (and modern) Middle East, hospitality embodied righteousness. Rebekah, the great-niece of Abraham, demonstrates that she is the "appointed" by her acts of hospitality.

The convergence of the trust in God's steadfast love and Rebekah's practice of hospitality brings fulfillment to this story. In contrast to the detailed telling of the servant's time with Rebekah's family, the writer of Genesis relates the meeting of Isaac and Rebekah in broad and tender strokes. As Rebekah draws one veil to cover her face, the servant lifts another by informing Isaac what has transpired. Then the veil of Sarah's tent closes upon Rebekah and Isaac. The text's only comment is that Isaac loved Rebekah and found comfort in the wake of his mother's death.

Will love's respite last forever? No. Children eventually will quarrel; parents ultimately will play favorites. The outcome of their love depends upon their choices. This is true of the caretaking of our loves. But this text insists that we remember that the genesis of love resides in God's providence. To say that love graces life is as much a statement of theology as emotion. The providential origin of Isaac's love is made explicit in the servant's search for the "appointed." Covenant is sustained not through merely securing a wife but through gracing life with love.

Consider your own life. Do you experience love's presence as sheer coincidence or as a providential gift of God's grace? Once we perceive love to flow from providence, from God's own *hesed* for us, then we may rightly cherish the loves with which God graces our lives and find joy in the respite love brings.

For Meditation This Day

O God, how much you must love me to grace my life with those I love. Renew my life in all love that comes as a gift from you.

~

Monday

Genesis 25:19-26   Signs of Things to Come

"If it is to be this way, why do I live?"

IDEALLY, GREAT HOPE AND PROMISE accompany pregnancy. The sense of new life's stirring within the womb may generate marvel and mystery and spark the wonder of parents who, with today's technology, can watch the flickering image of an ultrasound profile head and heart and fetal curl.

We do not know if Rebekah experienced the forming of new life within her with such joyful awe; the text is silent at that point. It only indicates that conception gave rise to struggle, and that struggle was the basis of Rebekah's poignant protest: "If it is to be this way...." In speaking those words, Rebekah may well be the first of Israel's prophets. Even before she inquires of God, Rebekah seems to grasp the meaning of what she feels growing inside: the way of struggle, of contention, of division between siblings.

Further events confirm Rebekah's apprehension. God declares the severity of division within her: two nations and two peoples of unequal strength. The greatest surprise, however, is God's revelation that the elder will serve the younger. What clashes within Rebekah is an overturning of tradition, a reversal of the normal order. Without explanation, God affirms the primacy of the younger. That this reversal will not come without contention finds illustration in the birthing itself. The ruddy first child cannot shake himself free from the grip of his younger twin who hangs on to the elder's heel. Thus does Genesis introduce Esau ("red" and "hairy") and Jacob ("he takes by the heel" or "he supplants").

"If it is to be this way, why do I live?" One may hear the compassion of a loving parent filtering through these words—a parent who would rather suffer herself than see strife and pain enter the lives of her children, a parent who would prefer death to enduring the ache of "if it is to be this way."

It is precisely at this point that the text is most vexing, yet most challenging. Clearly, things are to be this way. The text does not provide any quick or painless answers as to why—no endearing traits for Jacob or dastardly qualities of Esau justify the way it is to be for these two. Search as we might, neither our curiosity nor our sense of justice finds conclusive prooftext.

What we will find, however, is both the hint and challenge of grace. Its hint comes in God's choice of Jacob—without merit, without benefit of primogeniture (the right of the eldest to inherit). Its challenge comes in discerning where grace must be found: in the world as it is. When Rebekah considered "if it is to be this way"—in the world around her, in the world within her—she wondered, *Why live?* No grace came into sight, only struggle and conflict. Why bother?

The same may prove true for us. If in looking at the world we only see cause for resignation and despair, we probably will be resigned and despairing people. But if in this world, even within its struggles and conflicts, we can discern the birthing of grace—albeit in unlikely places and persons—then we may hope. We may hope that this world and its ways are not destined to remain the same forever. Why? Because of the grace that struggled against tradition and "the way things are" for birth within Rebekah's womb...the same grace with which God stirs this world toward new life.

For Meditation This Day

When I am tempted to throw up my hands in defeat, lift up my spirit in hope that I may see your grace newborn.

~~

Tuesday

Genesis 25:27-28   When Love Divides

Isaac loved Esau,...but Rebekah loved Jacob.

PERHAPS IT IS INEVITABLE. SOME SMALL trait or some long-past experience tips a parent's scale ever so slightly toward one child in particular. In the best of circumstances, that special regard need not disrupt relationships with other children or spouse. One need not choose sides when affording love to all.

In other circumstances, however, that special regard can sow discord. Favor toward one can become a bludgeon used upon others: "Why can't you be more like...?" In excess, such preference withholds love from the child(ren) who fails to measure up. Members choose sides; family splits; bias parodies love. The birth of Esau and Jacob portended future struggle between the two. Now it would seem that struggle sucks the parents into its maelstrom—or do they help create it? Isaac loves Esau. Rebekah loves Jacob. Each parent has a favorite. What the text leaves unspoken is the fact that each parent neglects part of his and her own flesh and blood in the process of choosing sides.

Why would a parent do such a thing? Isaac's reason is his fondness for game, a natural match with Esau's skill in hunting. The text gives no reason for Rebekah's inclination toward Jacob. Perhaps it arose from watching her husband dote on Esau, particularly when he longed for the smell of roasted wild meat dripping its fat upon the cookfire. Or perhaps it traced back to God's assertion to her that the younger would rule the elder—and Rebekah chose to cast her lot with a sure winner.

The reasons are almost incidental to the story. Isaac and Rebekah would be hard-pressed to justify withholding love from the other child on the basis of such reasoning. But then, I suspect that would be true of more contemporary rationalizations for parents favoring one offspring over another. Such reasons might explain the origin of favor, but they rarely if ever excuse the resulting disfavor.

And so Isaac and Rebekah practice a love that stamps the imprint of estrangement upon their children. Genesis never records a single conversation or encounter between Esau and Rebekah. As for Jacob and Isaac, their next meeting takes place under the guise of deception plotted by Rebekah and enacted by her favored one. Love divides, rather than creates, this family.

The story is a cautionary one, warning against the exercise of partiality in a parent's love. Yet in the very humanity of its characters, the narrative enables us to find our place within its action—and our own need for God's impartial love.

Parents can identify with the struggle to maintain love for all of one's children. That struggle may even intensify as children grow older. The matching of Esau's hunting with Isaac's hungering may mirror ways in which one child comes closer to matching a parent's desires and interests over passing years. But the closeness of one child ought not become excuse for dismissing another. Genuine love that makes room in the family for all at birthing times keeps room in the family for all through lifetimes.

Hidden away among the lines of this text is the movement of God's own gracious love. Those whom we trust to love us unconditionally will sometimes fail. Those who trust us to love them impartially will sometimes be disappointed. But we may trust God's love—a love that, for gracious reasons, elevates the younger over the elder; yet a love that embraces both Jacob and Esau. God's grace holds the mystery of this choice even as grace enables God's loving of both. And one day that grace will seek reconciliation for two brothers whom love now divides.

For Meditation This Day
Help me know your love, for that is the one thing I share in common with all who live; and in knowing, help me so to love.

Genesis 26:1-33   **Promises Kept**

"You [Isaac] are now the blessed of the Lord."

L IKE FATHER, LIKE SON, SO THE SAYING GOES. Much of
chapter 26, though told of Isaac, intentionally evokes
remembrances of Abraham. A famine sparks the movement of both (12:10; 26:1). Words of God's promised blessing
fall on both. As Abraham feared for his safety and twice passed
off Sarah as sister rather than wife (12:11-20; 20:1-18), so does
Isaac's fear cause him to attempt a similar ruse with Rebekah
(26:7-11). As Abraham disputed over a well at Beersheba but
eventually entered into a covenant with his former adversary
(21:25-32), so does Isaac do the same—ironically, at the same
site (26:15-33).

It might seem that Isaac never emerges from beneath his
father's shadow. In terms of sheer amount of material, the Abraham stories greatly outnumber those told of Isaac. Biblical
scholars point out that chapter 26 is the only chapter where
Isaac himself carries out the drama's action. Elsewhere, Isaac is
either acted upon (by Abraham—22:1-14), acted on behalf of
(by his father's servant—24:2-66), or acted against (by Rebekah
and Jacob—27:5-27).

In chapter 26, however, one theme does emerge that appears
to provide Isaac with his own identity within the covenant tradition. More than Abraham, Isaac is the one for whom God's
promised blessings find fulfillment within his lifetime. In verses 12-14, the blessings of material prosperity find lavish
description. Even though Abraham's wealth had been affirmed

earlier (13:2), what dominate the Abraham stories are God's promises of what will yet be—promises that first called Abraham to, and then sustained him on, a life of sojourn and hope. God announces such promises to Isaac as well (26:3-4, 24), but more than for his father they come to pass in Isaac's prosperity.

God's grace may take form in the richness with which one can enjoy and share life's blesssings. Such richness is not the obscene possession of more than one can ever use but richness as an overflowing of life's goodness. Such richness reflects the Hebrew understanding of *shalom*, a word that occurs twice in the close of this narrative (26:29, 31). *Shalom* comes closest in literal meaning to wholeness. The peace it signifies represents the presence of all things that make for well-being in life. In the text, the prosperity that blesses Isaac's life spills over into the peace shared with neighbors and former adversaries.

Peace, like prosperity, can move from promise to fulfillment. *Shalom* is not always a distant hope held on to against all odds—*shalom* binds Isaac to Abimelech at the place called Beersheba. The text and Isaac's place in the litany of God's covenant partners remind us that moments do come when God graces life with fulfillment as well as promise.

We do not always live in the realm of promise. Sometimes grace unfolds in our presence. Sometimes promises come to pass in our sight. Every time we confess faith in the God of Abraham and Isaac, we may remember that. And every time we experience that unfolding, we may give thanks for promises kept.

For Meditation This Day
When prosperity comes, remind me of more than my hard work or sheer luck—remind me of your grace and *shalom*.

Week Five

Unlikely Choices

Thursday

Genesis 27:1-38   Deceivers and Deceived

*"Your brother came deceitfully, and
he has taken away your blessing."*

I F THE NEAR-SACRIFICE OF ISAAC reveals something of the mystery of God's ways, then the tales swirling around Jacob raise questions about the fairness and justice of those ways.

Of all the characters that the Book of Genesis identifies as patriarchs and matriarchs of the promise, none is so ethically objectionable as Jacob—Jacob the opportunist, who earlier seized upon Esau's hunger as a means to secure the elder's birthright; Jacob the swindler, who with his mother's help carries out this grand deception of a blind father to receive words of blessing intended for Esau.

Yet God chooses this Jacob—Jacob the favored, set apart by God from before birth to rule his elder brother; Jacob the promise-bearer, heir to the vows God made to faithful Abraham and obedient Isaac. Faithfulness and obedience seem alien to the character of Jacob as he dons Esau's clothes and lies to Isaac. Where is the fairness of God's setting aside the traditional rights of the elder for this deceitful younger? Where is God's justice in the midst of Jacob's compounding treacheries? And where does one find the grace of God in the twists and turns of this narrative and its primary character?

These larger questions do not find resolution within the confines of the saga of Jacob's and Rebekah's deception of Isaac (and defrauding of Esau). Instead, we catch glimpses of a family turned upon itself. Isaac, still partial to Esau's "savory food" (27:4), puts his desire for food before blessing. So instructed,

Friday

Genesis 27:41–28:5   The Search for Sanctuary

"Why should I lose both of you in one day?"

S ANCTUARY: A PLACE OF WORSHIP, a place of refuge. The first recipient of sanctuary as refuge in Genesis had been Cain, lest the murderer of his brother become the murdered. Now Jacob becomes the seeker of sanctuary, lest the defrauder of his brother become the murdered.

Actually Rebekah sets Jacob on the quest for sanctuary, directing her younger son to flee to her own family's home. Ironically, Rebekah herself seeks sanctuary in Jacob's journey: sanctuary from more unwise marital choices by her sons. The Hittite wives of Esau had grieved his parents no end (26:35). Her lament to Isaac about that situation moves him to charge Jacob to find a wife from Rebekah's nieces. Even the search for sanctuary comes with the mixed motives of Jacob's safety and his parents' desire for domestic tranquility.

On the surface, the text contains little grace and much manipulation. Esau plots revenge at Isaac's death. Rebekah rests her hopes for Jacob's eventual return in the failing of Esau's memory. Isaac and Rebekah dictate Jacob's journey.

As was true in the narrative of Jacob's deception of Isaac, God is now neither invoked by the characters nor manifest in their actions. Between the lines, however, providence moves. Where Esau waits for the right time to strike back, God will use the passage of time to reconcile. Where Rebekah counts on forgetfulness to enable return, God will rely on remembrance to pave the way for reunion. Where Isaac and Rebekah script Jacob's journey for him, God will journey with him. Where

Jacob seeks sanctuary to hide, God will confront Jacob within sanctuary so that he may find himself.

That expansion of the notion of sanctuary from place of refuge to encounter with the holy—and ourselves—frames not only Jacob's impending journey but our own. Consider the places you associate with sanctuary in your life: a church, a home, a mountain vista, a streamside park, a stark desert. Whatever the setting, sanctuary affords a respite from pressing schedules and simmering turmoils: a refuge from those things that besiege us. Yet if sanctuary is escape and nothing more, it is not sanctuary. For sanctuary also bears with it the experience and presence of power and life greater than our own.

As the name suggests, sanctuary is the place where we find ourselves sanctified: set apart, called, challenged, graced. The design or appearance of sanctuary is not nearly as important for us as its function. Sanctuary is the place where we encounter God, the place where we encounter our true selves. And since the God we worship is the God of grace, the gift of sanctuary is a gift of grace. That means, among other things, that we may experience sanctuary in totally unexpected places and unanticipated persons. As with Jacob, our search for sanctuary's refuge may have to first confront us with who we are so grace may enable us to see who we may yet be.

Did Rebekah and Isaac understand that when they sent Jacob packing? The text does not indicate that they did, nor does it provide any hint that Jacob did. Yet that is the beauty of God's grace: We need not set out intentionally in search of it to be found by it. Even when our own search for sanctuary proceeds with mixed motives, God may still find a way to touch us in saving and life-changing ways we never imagined. So it was with Jacob. So it may be with us.

For Meditation this Day

God, lead me to those places of sanctuary where I may find you; that in coming to you, I may come to myself.

~◦

Saturday

Genesis 28:10-17   **The Ladder**

And he dreamed that there was a ladder set up on
the earth, the top of it reaching to heaven.

HAVE YOU EVER HEARD THE WARNING: Be careful what you pray for; you just might get it? Jacob may or may not have used prayer as ably as he had used deception in obtaining Isaac's blessing, but obtain the blessing he did. Jacob got just what he wanted.

Or did he? Perhaps Jacob might have considered his desires more carefully had he known the consequences. Everything he wanted proved to have more strings attached and more fine print involved than he or Rebekah ever imagined. The blessing that had required the very best (worst) of his talents suddenly became Jacob's curse. All the elements of his father's blessing—land, family, domination—became ironic memory. Jacob had to leave all behind to flee for his life. The word of blessing degenerated into a writ of exile.

Jacob flees for Haran. Yet in Jacob's isolation, when scheming and cunning will be of no avail should Esau find him, God confronts Jacob. The confrontation comes in a dream, a time when the mind's defenses are down. The dream depicts a ladder with angels ascending and descending. Such imagery provides a graphic portrayal of this world's inextricable link to the heavenly realm of God. Jacob might pull the wool over a blind father's eyes, but his actions cannot escape the attention of the God whose angels move freely between this earth and heaven. Yet rather than using the dream and its ladder binding heaven and earth to upbraid Jacob for his questionable activities, they become the vehicle for assuring Jacob of God's promises. Beyond a restatement of the familiar pledges of descendants and land and blessing, the dream conveys a fresh word of promise: "I am with you and will keep you wherever you go, and will bring you back to this land."

The extraordinary nature of God's promise becomes clear when contrasted with Jacob's current situation. Jacob, removed from the company of all who loved—and hated—him, is offered the presence of God ("I am with you"). Jacob, fleeing for his life that is no longer within his own capabilities to defend, is offered the protective sheltering of God ("I will keep you wherever you go"). Jacob, the one who carries the blessing but not the possession of land and home, is offered homecoming by God ("I will bring you back to this land").

Jacob will receive all that he had schemed and deceived to gain. Only now it is not a matter of seized opportunity but of patient waiting. Jacob will not obtain it by relying on all the tricks in the book but by relying on the Promise-Maker. Jacob's God will be a God of grace, just as this God was for Abraham and Isaac—and, in an odd way, for Esau. We see grace not only in the unlikely choice of Jacob but in the means by which these promises will unfold.

At the moment of Jacob's first awakening, the dream has its intended impact. Jacob acknowledges the Lord to be in this place, a truth he had not recognized when he lay down his head in sleep. Fear accompanies this recognition: fear perhaps generated not only by encounter with God but by Jacob's realization of his own unworthiness. "This is the gate of heaven," Jacob confesses. And this confession serves as the first of several turning points toward the grace that seeks transformation.

For Meditation this Day

Help me see the links that join this world and your heavenly realm, the links that join my life and your presence—and help me live in that joining.

~

Sunday

Genesis 28:18-22   **Bargaining with God**

If God will… , then the Lord shall be my God.

TIMES OF ILLNESS OR DANGER sometimes generate the equivalent of negotiations with God. If only this will pass, promises are made. By his own admission, Martin Luther's decision to enter religious orders came as the result of a nearby lightning strike while he was walking in a storm. He linked his cry for help to Saint Anne with a vow to become a monk.

Today's text portrays negotiations of a different sort. Awakening from his dream of the ladder and God's promises, Jacob anoints the stone on which he lay and names this place Beth-el: "House of God." But Jacob, who once bargained away Esau's birthright with a mere bowl of soup, sets his bartering stakes higher.

Before Jacob offers anything by way of faith or trust, he sets the conditions for relationship and covenant. "*If* God will be with me, *if* [God] will keep me… , *if* [God] will give me bread to eat and clothing to wear, so that I come again to my father's house in peace"—then, and only then, will the Lord be Jacob's God. It's as if Jacob is doing God a favor. And, as if to sweeten the pot for God's favor, Jacob vows to return a tenth of what God gives (28:22)

Once again, we are back to Jacob the soup salesman, the deal-maker. Even after the dream, even after the promises, Jacob is not yet ready to turn loose his life in trust. Like his New Testament cousin in spirit Thomas, Jacob will have to see with his own eyes and touch with his own hands how God keeps God's end of the bargain. If you do these things, then you shall be my God.

The chosen one of God does not quite know what to do with that chosenness yet. Jacob still wants to get all that he can by his own devices, while God simply wants to give. Jacob attaches conditions and prices to relationship and covenant, while God offers grace.

And what of us? In what ways is our faith a set of conditions we impose on God, waiting to see if God is equal to our task? In the ensuing stories from the Hebrew Scriptures, idolatry—the fashioning of god(s) in human likeness—looms as a major threat to the covenant relationship. But what of that idolatry that seeks not so much to fashion God in our likeness as to redefine God as the One who fulfills our wants and desires? the idolatry where we would remake God not in our own image but as our own personal benefactor?

The problem with such efforts, whether our own or Jacob's, is that they do not allow God's grace to reign in our lives. They assume that either we know better than God what is best for us or that God will not do good for us unless coerced to do so. Do we really believe either of those? Or have we become so used to fending for ourselves that we find it hard to trust God's gracious keeping of our lives?

For Jacob, the question remains unanswered for now. The text records no reply from God to Jacob's attempted bargain.

And for us? The reliance upon grace reveals itself every time we turn down the temptation to negotiate God's meeting our desires in place of trusting God's promises to supply our needs. We cannot bargain for grace: It can only be offered and received.

For Meditation This Day
Remind me, O God, that you already offer all that I need. When I would bargain, teach me to trust in you and in grace.

~

Monday

Genesis 29:15-30   **The Deceiver Deceived**

"What is this you have done to me?"

WHAT GOES AROUND COMES AROUND." Those words might serve as an alternate heading to this day's reading. The one who forged his seizure of a father's promise by deceit now finds himself the victim of a father-in-law's cunning. The deceiver is deceived.

As a whole, the Jacob-Laban stories provide curiously comic relief to the narrative. Jacob, the archetype of Samson, rolls away a well stone to impress Rachel (29:2, 10). Jacob, the nervous bridegroom, incredibly fails to realize he spends his wedding night with his intended's sister. Laban, the master of timely disclosure, reveals only then that the older daughter must precede the younger in marriage. Laban, the aggrieved, searches in vain for his stolen household gods while Rachel calmly sits atop them, compounding the indignity by claiming this as being the time when "the way of women" is upon her (31:34-35).

Central to all, however, is Laban's deception of Jacob. Seven years does Isaac's son labor for his uncle, all for the sake of

Rachel...and seven years more, when the morning after the wedding brings its surprise. On one level, we may read the story simply as Jacob's comeuppance: Jacob experiences first-hand what it means to be cheated. There is a certain poetic justice to Jacob's finally reaping what he has sown—but what of grace? May we find its glimpses and traces here?

Something new about Jacob appears in this text. For the first time in Genesis, Jacob is not self-absorbed, advancing his own agenda. The reason is his love for Rachel—a love that enables Jacob to give Laban seven years of his life; a love that, in an extraordinary act, moves Jacob to invest seven more years of his service to the very one who deceived him.

Is love the same as grace? Not necessarily. But love without conditions, love offered regardless of the cost, love that accepts whatever is necessary to achieve its purposes: Such love hints of, if not embodies, grace. And one of the most unlikely of persons to show such love is Jacob; yet he does. Even Laban's deceit does not dissuade Jacob. The one previously known for bargaining birthrights and swindling blessings and attempting to strike deals with God now is the one who loves with tenacity.

To love with tenacity. Such a description fits well with the gracious love of God revealed throughout Genesis, whether it be love bestowed on a human creation whose post-Flood heart is still evil from youth or love maintained for a scheming upstart whose treatment of brother and father seems love's very antithesis. To love with tenacity rings true to the heart of this Lenten season: a love that journeys on toward Jerusalem and cross undeterred, the same love from which nothing will be able to separate us.

Make no mistake; Jacob's journey is far from done. There is still some of the schemer left. But something has happened; Jacob has changed—and for the better. After learning of the deceit, Jacob cried to Laban: "What is this you have done to me?" Jacob might have directed those words toward God, for God had done something with Jacob…and God wasn't through yet.

And if God's grace can bring change to the likes of Jacob, what of you, what of me? "What is this you have done to me?" We might ask the same of God, for the grace of God is doing something with us . . . and God isn't through with us yet.

For Meditation This Day

O God, sometimes you work in strange ways and through strange persons—but always you work by grace and love. Help me do the same.

~

Tuesday

Genesis 32:22-32   **New Name, New Identity**

"You shall no longer be called Jacob, but Israel."

THE STORY OF JACOB'S WRESTLING provides an episode whose various supernatural elements are uncommon to the biblical materials. Some would tame the wildness of the text by passing it off as a legendary tale of Canaanite demons that found its way into the Jacob cycle of stories. Others would rationalize it by approaching it as a psychological study of Jacob's inner turmoils generated by the imminence of reunion with Esau. But what if we simply allow the story to speak for itself?

The text never absolutely discloses the man's identity. One popular assumption is that the man is an angel. The more disquieting possibility is that it is God. Jacob himself calls this place Peniel, "the face of God": "For I have seen God face to face." Is Jacob mistaken? Or is the scandal of an earthy, wrestling God too much for the author to preserve definitively in writing?—a scandal made all the more exceptional by the match's outcome: a draw.

When day is about to break, it is the man who seeks an end to the wrestling. At that moment, the old Jacob appears: "I will not let you go, unless you bless me." Wounded Jacob can still see an opportunity to extract blessing, this time by force rather than deceit. But, as was the case with his father's blessing, Jacob gets more than he bargained for: not simply a new blessing but a new name—Israel, "one who strives with God" or "God strives." Either interpretation would be true. The night of wrestling showed Jacob to be capable of contending with God. And the years of working and waiting upon Jacob showed God to be capable of striving to see the promises fulfilled, even in the likes of Jacob-now-Israel.

Names played a critical role among the Hebrews and other peoples of the ancient Near East. Names often bestowed or anticipated something of that person's identity. Jacob, whose name meant "one who supplants" or "heel," certainly lived up to such an identity on both accounts. Yet over the course of his life, the "heel" became Israel, "the one who strives with God." How?

The identity switch results from Jacob's willingness to trust God. Remember that the wrestling occurs after Jacob decides to return home. God had kept all of God's promises to Jacob except one: to bring Jacob back. And that promise depended upon Jacob's willingness to trust God for safekeeping. Even though Jacob still feared Esau (32:11), he made the difficult decision of setting out for home. The "supplanter" and "heel" were gone. So God graced Jacob with a new name.

Have you ever wrestled with God? We may be hard-pressed to describe such encounters in the graphic terms of Genesis. Yet it is difficult to conceive of coming to maturity of faith without some contention. Perhaps the struggle is over injustice in the world and why God allows it or suffering or confusion over directions to go and choices to make. Perhaps, as in Jacob's story, the wrestling issues from the tension between the risk of trusting God and our bent toward self-reliance. What happens when you encounter situations where resolution or reconciliation ultimately reside beyond your power to manipulate or control?

Jacob's wrestling with God resulted in the gracing of his life with a new name and a new identity. What of our wrestling with God? Do we fear the very idea of contending with God, thinking it an impious act? Or do we discover in such striving that God still brings blessing, gracing us with new identities through faith tempered in such contending.

For Meditation This Day
Grant me persistence as I struggle to see your ways, O God, and grace me with endurance as I struggle to follow in them.

~⁀○

Genesis 33:1-11   **Seeing the Face of God**

"To see your face is like seeing the face of God."

I N WHOM DO WE SEE THE FACE OF GOD? Many may
glimpse God in the face of one we love and whose love
renews and freshens our life. For some, the sight might
arise in the face of one of the least of these our brothers and
sisters, a seeing generated by serving in Christ's stead and
heeding Christ's admonition. Others, either out of a despair
that conceives of the world as God-bereft or a rigid piety that
excludes the possibility of ever looking upon the face of God
in the things of a fallen creation, cannot see God.

These are all likely answers to the question of where and in
whom we may see the face of God. However, in the last of these
reflections on God's unlikely choices, an equally unlikely answer
to that same question takes form.

As the narrative makes clear here and before (32:1-21),
Jacob takes extraordinary precautions. Jacob has no illusions
about a sentimental reunion awaiting him, particularly when
word reaches him that Esau approaches with four hundred
men (32:6). To curry Esau's favor, Jacob sends presents (32:13-
21). To prepare for Esau's wrath, Jacob twice divides his ret-
inue into separate groups (32:7-8; 33:1-2). Whereas the old
Jacob might have cowered behind those who traveled with him
to assess Esau's intent, Jacob stands at the head of his wives
and children to meet his brother.

Listen to the chain of events; see if they remind you of another story whose theme is grace. Jacob returns to his brother,

bowing in humility. But Esau—Esau runs and embraces him, kissing him and weeping. Does that not call to mind another scene: "But while he was still far off, his father saw him and was filled with compassion; he ran and put his arms around him and kissed him" (Luke 15:20). Jacob the prodigal returns home, not to the expected vengeance or retribution of an enemy but to the unexpected love and embrace of his brother.

In their ensuing dialogue, Jacob twice connects his sending of presents as an attempt to find favor with Esau. The Hebrew word for "favor" is *chen*; its alternate translation is "grace." The same grace (*chen*) that Noah and Abraham found with God (6:8; 18:3) is the grace Jacob sought through gifts. Yet Esau tells Jacob he has enough, which is to say that the presents have nothing to do with his coming to meet Jacob. Esau's grace toward Jacob is not a transaction: It is a gift—grace tucked away in the quiet but revealing fact of Esau's calling Jacob "my brother" (33:9).

Imagine what Esau could have called Jacob: my supplanter, from Jacob's naming; my deceiver, from Jacob's action; my lord, from Jacob's destiny. Yet Esau calls Jacob the one name no one else could: my brother. Grace restores relationship.

And Jacob, the long-time beneficiary of God's unexplained grace, looks into the face of the one he dreaded and feared and avoided—and recognizes that same grace. "To see your face is like seeing the face of God—since you have received me with such favor [*chen*]" (33:10). Seeing the face of Esau *is* like seeing the face of God; Jacob receives grace from both.

And so we return to where we began: In whom do we see the face of God? The unlikely answer, echoed in God's own unlikely choice of Jacob, is anyone. Anyone from whom we find ourselves encountering grace: grace in unmerited forgiveness, grace in unexpected reconciliation, grace in unconditional love. Like Jacob, may we recognize the face of God among us. And like Esau, may we serve as the face of God for those in need of grace.

For Meditation This Day

Give me eyes and spirit to perceive your grace among persons in my daily life, and give me life and faith to embody your grace for others.

~

Week Six

~

Irrepressible Providence

Thursday

Genesis 37:1-11   **From Shlimazel to Dreamer**

When his brothers saw that their father loved [Joseph] more than all his brothers, they hated him....And when [Joseph] told [his dream] to his brothers, they hated him even more.

SOME YEARS AGO, I CAME ACROSS THIS description of the difference between a *shlemiel* and a *shlimazel,* two expressive Yiddish words. A *shlemiel* is the kind of person who, at public gatherings, invariably spills his or her cup or coffee or soup. This is the classic bumbler, much like Peter Sellers' character Inspector Clouseau in the Pink Panther movies. A *shlimazel,* on the other hand, is the kind of person at those same gatherings upon whom the coffee or soup is spilled. Through no seeming fault of their own, *shlimazels* are the inevitable victims.

At first glance, one might write Joseph off as the Genesis version of the *shlimazel.* Through no fault—and no quality—of his own, Joseph is preferred by Jacob to all his other brothers. Yet Joseph, not Jacob, bears the brunt of his brothers' outrage. As a sign of his favor, Jacob gives Joseph a long robe with sleeves. His brothers bring home the tattered and bloodied remains of that same robe to convince Jacob that wild beasts have devoured his favorite son. Through their deception, they seek to conceal the ugly truth: They have sold their own kin to slave traders.

Even after his arrival in Egypt, Joseph finds himself wearing a lapful of somebody else's soup. His honorable declining of seduction by Potiphar's wife lands him in Pharaoh's prison. His interpreting of a fellow prisoner's dream that comes to pass leads not to Joseph's elevation but to his continued disregard...but this is getting ahead of the story. Joseph always seems to be the innocent victim, the *shlimazel*. Or is he?

The one common thread that weaves its way through the Joseph narrative is not that he is Jacob's favorite or that he is the owner of a special garment that makes him look (and perhaps at times act) like a strutting peacock before his brothers. No, the common thread twisting its way through brotherly hate, unjust imprisonment, and the heights of power stems from the fifth verse of chapter 37: "Once Joseph had a dream"—a dream of stars and moon and sun bowing down before Joseph, a dream that discloses Joseph's rule though not the reasons why. From the perspective of Genesis, Joseph is neither victim nor *shlimazel*. He is, first and foremost, a dreamer.

Do you begin to see what is at work here? It's not really Jacob's favor or the robe with sleeves that turns this family, and eventually the house of Pharaoh, upside down. It is the grace of God: a grace that selects Joseph, a grace that works through—of all things—dreams...and dreamer.

Maybe it is not so surprising to find grace lurking in dreams and in those who give them credence. Dreams do not always speak of current reality; dreams take persons out of the ordinary realms of life and grant them a vision of new places. And consider dreamers: Dreamers are apt to take those things and those new places seriously. Dreamers are liable to see connections between the routine and the possible, between what everyone understands to be a given and what may yet be given.

So the irrepressible providence of God pokes its head into the narrative and into Joseph's life through a dream. What unfolds is not the victimization of Joseph the *shlimazel* but the providential care of Joseph the dreamer.

For Meditation This Day

God, what dreams do you give me? And how, by your grace, do I keep faith with those dreams when they—and I—are sorely tested?

~⌒

Friday

Genesis 37:12-36   **On the Killing of Dreams**

"Here comes this dreamer. Come now, let us kill him…and we shall see what will become of his dreams."

I T IS STRANGE THE WAY WE DISMISS PEOPLE we judge to be powerless or ineffective by calling them dreamers. The Joseph stories reveal that dreams bear great power, even as those who receive dreams may incite great hostility. At least, dreams have that capacity when they are affirmed.

Joseph could have defused the situation by dismissing his dream as childish imagining, never to share it with anyone. Or, if for some reason he felt the need to convey the dream's details to his brothers, he could have done so by ridiculing its idea of elders serving younger. Joseph the dreamer would then have been no threat to them. No harm comes from dreams, so long as those to whom they are given consider them as no more than fantasy.

In 1963 one man addressed hundreds of thousands of people with a different sort of a dream—yet it was a dream that stirred hostility, as Joseph's dream had done. Had Martin Luther King, Jr., been content to dream in the quiet of the pastoral study or in the safety of close circles of friends or even limited it to liturgies recited within sanctuaries, his dream would have remained eloquent; but it would have been impotent. Instead,

King took the dream to the streets. He applied its vision to bus drivers and sanitation workers and war protestors. Belief in the dream led to the dream's enacting. Unlike Jacob, King's father did not receive a tattered remnant of cloth. A casket bore his dreamer home.

Now it would have caused Martin far less trouble, his family far less anxiety, his father far less grief, had Martin dismissed his dream as idealistic wishes for what could never be. Instead, Martin Luther King's dream became the beacon toward which he lived.

From both Martin and Joseph, we learn that the task of the dreamer is that of maintaining integrity—maintaining integrity to the dream, integrity to its Giver, integrity to holding faith and action in balance. Beyond that, sustaining the dream involves patient trust in the providence of God. Evidence of fulfillment is nice, but it is not always forthcoming. Conflicting testimony about the dream's reality and practicality always abounds. Precisely in those times of waiting and testing, the dreams of God for the people of God prove their (and our) worth. The dream given Joseph bears its greatest potential for change not when Joseph prospers, but when he sits alone and abandoned. Martin's dream offers its greatest hope for reconciliation not when blacks and whites and browns and reds sit down together at tables of fellowship, but when we stand alienated from and at odds with one another.

When God's providence is hardest to see, faith comes to the forefront—faith that keeps integrity to the dreams God entrusts to us; faith that determines to enact those dreams; faith that understands, by hope in God's providence, its dreams will not be lost in slavery or prison or perish with bullets or crosses. For faith trusts that its dreams, even when given up for dead, will rise.

The tomb of Martin Luther King, Jr., gives testimony to such faith. Engraved there for all who come as pilgrims or simply the curious is the witness of Genesis 37:19-20: "Here comes this dreamer. Come now, let us kill him…, and we shall see what will become of his dreams."

We shall see by our further reading what became of the dream given to Joseph. We shall see by our further living what becomes of Martin's dream. What becomes of dreams is not only what we make of them but what God makes of us through them!

For Meditation This Day
Lord, do I set aside your dreams when others object? Steady me when dreams delay; anchor me when objections hurt.

~⊃

Saturday

Genesis 39:1-23   **Loyalty or Convenience**

*"How then could I do this great wickedness,
and sin against God?"*

DURING MY STUDENT YEARS AT EDEN Seminary in St. Louis, Dr. Robert Bertram taught Christian ethics at nearby Concordia Seminary. In that course, which several of us from Eden attended, he offered this concise yet telling definition: "Ethics is what you do in a strange city where no one knows who you are." When the fear of public disclosure is eliminated, how one chooses to act relies upon one's inner character. Even if others do not know who you are, you know who you are. Loyalty to oneself provides a key to integrity of character.

Esau goes to hunt. Rebekah, still partial to Jacob, crafts a plan to obtain the blessing intended for Esau. So instructed, Jacob goes to deceive.

Rebekah might have claimed that she simply wished to fulfill what God had revealed about the destiny of the twins. Jacob might have offered that same justification—though his being the beneficiary would have cast a long shadow upon his objectivity. It is telling, however, that the narrative leading up to the blessing contains no invocation or revelation of God's direction. For Jacob and Rebekah, Isaac's blessing was an opportunity to seize, rather than a gift to receive. Snatching the benediction was worth any cost...and the cost proved dear.

And what of the deceived? Isaac seems to be a helpless victim: blind, aged, thinking of his own death. But delve more deeply into the story and you see that Isaac is equally to blame for Esau's defrauding. Isaac places satisfying his hunger before blessing his elder. With sight gone, Isaac puts his trust in the physical senses of touch and smell and taste. His hearing alerts him to deceit (27:22). A parent would know a child's voice, a voice heard from birth through youth into adulthood, a voice embodied in the gift of relationship. It is the sense most difficult to deceive. But such doubts dissolve in the filling of Isaac's stomach and the smell of the field on stolen clothes.

So Esau returns from the field, hands full of food for Isaac; but Isaac's hands hold no blessing. Esau receives only tears. So the narration of God's unlikely choices begin with this family of deceivers and deceived.

For Meditation this Day
Forgive me, O God, when I presume the future is mine to make at the expense of others—and of you.

~

Joseph was a stranger in a strange land, sold into slavery by his own brothers. In spite of this predicament, the grace of God shows itself clearly in the story's opening. God's presence with Joseph results in his rise among the household servants of Potiphar, his owner. The more responsibility Potiphar delegates to Joseph, the more God brings blessing upon the Egyptian's house. Three times the text asserts that Potiphar entrusted Joseph with charge over "all that he had" (39:4, 5, 6). So when Potiphar's wife suggests a sexual liaison with her husband's favored servant, Joseph faces an ethical dilemma.

An ethic of convenience would pose no problem with such an affair. The pleasure of the moment might also secure Joseph some future favor from someone able to advance his interests. An ethic based on duty or social obligation would also offer an excuse for the proposed intrigue. As a servant, Joseph was compelled to heed his superior's wishes. Joseph might have rationalized this course of action, saying he had no real choice given his position. Joseph could also have invoked an ethics of "what others don't know can't hurt you"—what you do in a strange city where no one knows you. If Joseph could secure a promise of secrecy from Potiphar's wife, he might avoid disclosure and no one would be the wiser. No one, that is, save Joseph.

Joseph rejects the offer out of his loyalty, not only to Potiphar but to God (39:8-9). "How then could I do this" traces back to the relationship of trust that exists between Joseph and his master and to Joseph's understanding that such an act would constitute sin against God. Joseph operates from an ethic of loyalty: loyalty to Potiphar, loyalty to God. And loyalty to others hinges on loyalty to oneself. How can one be consistent in relationships with others if one's own self-image and standards are of two minds: one for public consumption and one for private indulgence? Joseph as faithful servant, whether of God or Potiphar, derives from Joseph as person of integrity.

Rage (39:19), however, overlooks reality and ignores loyalty. As a consequence of his faithfulness, Joseph finds himself unfairly accused and unjustly imprisoned. Now the text does go on to declare that God continues to support Joseph in prison with God's steadfast love (39:21-23). But consider this: If we learned no more of Joseph after his being thrown into prison, how would we judge his loyalty to God and Potiphar and self? Would we see Joseph as naive, not understanding that "to get along you have to go along?" Would we judge Joseph as tragic for not realizing that one cannot fight the powers that be? The answer depends on where (or if) we locate the working of grace in this narrative.

Grace emerges here not only in the ultimate unfolding of good in this story, but in Joseph's initial choice to act with loyalty. Our loyalty to God finds its beginning in God's loyalty to us: God's steadfast love stands by us through changing fortunes. May we find our strength in grace that empowers human integrity, as evidenced in Joseph. And when our loyalty to God and self proves less than that shown by Joseph, may we also find our hope in grace that forgives human failure.

For Meditation This Day

O God, we pray for loyalty and integrity of heart and mind, through word and deed, in public and private, to you and neighbor.

~

Sunday

Genesis 40:1-23 **Forgotten**

The chief cupbearer did not remember Joseph, but forgot him.

ORGOTTEN. A CHILD LEFT BEHIND or left out in a game, a friend overlooked in a time of need, a spouse neglected at a birthday or anniversary. Have you ever experienced what it feels like to be forgotten? You move among others who do not seem to notice you—or in noticing, do not seem to care.

"Take care that you do not forget the Lord" (Deuteronomy 6:12; 8:11) forms a common theme in the Hebrew Scriptures. The reverse anxiety is that God might forget us: "Will you forget me forever?" (Psalm 13:1). "Why have you forgotten me?" (Psalm 42:9). Jesus' own cry of God-forsakenness on the cross echoes the ancient lament of Psalm 22:1. (See Matthew 27:46; Mark 15:34.)

To be forgotten, whether by God or another, creates a spiritual crisis. That point is critical to our understanding of what confronts Joseph. Joseph remained unjustly imprisoned, though God's steadfast love (*hesed*) for him resulted in Joseph's finding favor with the chief jailer. As a result, Joseph prospered even in these circumstances (Genesis 39:21-23).

When two new prisoners (former servants of Pharaoh) appear, the jailer entrusts their care to Joseph. Joseph apparently takes his commission seriously, asking them the cause for their troubled looks one morning. Dreams, they reply—to the dreamer. The dreams and their interpretations are as different as night and day. One portends success and restoration, the other judgment and death.

Joseph asks nothing of the baker whose dream presages doom. But the cupbearer's dream indicates his return to Pharaoh's trust. The office of cupbearer was a critical one in these times. Pharaoh could keep any number of armed men to protect him from harm brought by overt attack. But Pharaoh had to be able to trust the cupbearer, along with those who brought Pharaoh his food, absolutely. If conspirators sought to kill Pharaoh, poisoning involved the least risk of exposure. The cupbearer was no mere servant among many. Pharaoh would designate someone of unquestionable loyalty. Held in such confidence, the cupbearer would naturally have the ear of the king in other matters.

In Joseph's case, the hearing of such matters might lead to his freedom. "But remember me when it is well with you; please do me the kindness to make mention of me to Pharaoh, and so get me out of this place" (40:14). Joseph does not engage in wishful thinking in this request. The word of the cupbearer would hold great sway with Pharaoh: Who would not want to satisfy a simple request of one who stands between you and your enemies? So Joseph strikes his bargain. The providence of God has placed him in contact with the soon-to-be intimate of Pharaoh.

Things are looking up, except for one thing: "Yet the chief cupbearer did not remember Joseph, but forgot him" (40:23). Forgotten. Forgotten for two years, according to the time frame set by 41:1. Two whole years. Have you ever been forgotten for such a length of time? Forgotten, not just as in left alone—but as left in the sort of circumstances as Joseph finds himself in.

Consider times when you have sat by the phone waiting for a promised call. Seconds turn to minutes and more. Impatience rises; hope fades. Multiply that by two years. Multiply the anxiety of not hearing with not being free while you wait. And what if you could not resume your life until you were no longer forgotten? There we find Joseph at story's end—forgotten, imprisoned. And the latter will not change until the former is reversed. Due to human forgetfulness, grace must wait in the wings. Then and now.

For Meditation This Day

Do not forget me, O God; and do not let me forget you or others.

~~

Monday

Genesis 41:9-46   **Remembrance and Renewal**

*Then the chief cupbearer said to Pharaoh,
"I remember my faults today."*

THEY SAY THAT CONFESSION IS GOOD for the soul. The chief cupbearer's confession arises from remembrance of a fault—and a person—long forgotten. Pharaoh's dream that defies interpretation triggers the cupbearer's remembrance of his prison experience, probably a time he would rather forget. It was a time when a dream also had him baffled until a young Hebrew named Joseph offered an interpretation that had in fact come to pass. Now, in the face of Pharaoh's bewildering dream, the cupbearer remembers one who interprets dreams. It is the one he promised to remember to Pharaoh years before but forgot until now. And so the cupbearer remembers his faults by remembering Joseph.

Is it natural for remembrance of past sin or faults to summon memories of those against whom our choices or negligence fell hard? It is easy to remember and confess sin that weighs down upon our lives in its consequences. But what of our sin, our "faults," that seem to leave us unscathed while devastating others? A thoughtless word of gossip impugns another's reputation without sullying our own. A cutting word of hatred belittles someone's value without reflecting back on our own. Does confession of sin that forgets sin's victims count? Perhaps Jesus' command about leaving your gift at the altar in order first to be reconciled with your brother or sister (Matt. 5:23-24) hints that remembrance of persons takes precedence.

To his credit, Pharaoh's chief cupbearer links confession of his fault with remembrance of Joseph—remembrance that had, after all, been the only reward Joseph had asked of him. And with Joseph now remembered before Pharaoh, providence works to bring Joseph into Pharaoh's presence to interpret the dream. Ironically, Joseph also engages in remembrance. When Pharaoh declares his understanding that Joseph has the ability to interpret dreams, Joseph qualifies that by saying, "It is not I; God will give Pharaoh a favorable answer" (41:16). Joseph remembers the One from whom his gift of interpretation comes, thus setting the stage for remembrance to result in renewal.

The story of the dream and its interpretation unfolds: seven years of prosperity followed by seven years of famine. In verse 33, the text moves from Joseph's interpretation to his proposed strategy for dealing with the crisis. In that proposal (not simply the dream's interpretation), Pharaoh sees Joseph as filled with the spirit of God—an extraordinary confession of faith for a figure whom Egyptian tradition considered as deity himself. By the end of the text, the thirty-year-old Joseph has risen from prisoner to having no equal in Egypt save Pharaoh.

The incredible potential of God's grace and providence to

renew human life finds testimony in Joseph's ascent. The one forgotten is now the one empowered. The depths in which we may find ourselves at times do not have the final word over us.

God may yet find ways—and persons—in which to raise us and others up. And the ability of grace to use persons, even forgetful ones, reminds us of our own potential as instruments of God's grace to others. Our remembrance of the forgotten, not to mention our remembrance of those who have suffered because of our "faults," can become the means through which God brings renewal to their lives—and forgiveness to our own.

"The chief cupbearer said to Pharaoh, 'I remember...'" Whom do we need to remember? And by whose remembrance have we been lifted to newness of life?

For Meditation This Day
Whether in confession or thanksgiving, O God, help me to remember you and help me to remember others. And by your grace, remember me.

Tuesday

Genesis 45:1-15   **Power That Forgives**

"And now do not be distressed, or angry with yourselves,
...for God sent me before you to preserve life."

AFGHAN FORCES TOOK TWO ENGLISH colonial officers prisoner. Throughout their imprisonment, the officers kept a diary of their experiences in the margins of a prayer book. A third prisoner wrote the final entry in the book, stating the two officers had been led out, flogged, and then forced to dig two graves—never to be seen again.

Twenty-one years passed before a remarkable set of circumstances resulted in that prayer book's coming into the hands of the sister of one of the slain officers. Reading the entries convinced her that revenge was needed—Christian revenge. And the method settled upon? Taking all the money she could spare, she sent it to a British hospital in India. She enclosed instructions for its use: to keep a bed free for a sick or wounded Afghan and to care for him until health returned. This was to be done in memory of her brother*: An opportunity for revenge met by the commitment to forgive.

We encounter this same surprising and powerful theme with Joseph. The one sold by brothers, framed by Potiphar's wife, and forgotten by Pharaoh's cupbearer now stands in an enviable position to repay old debts. Nowhere is that potential to levy reprisal more clear than when those same brothers who cast Joseph into a pit come begging for food.

As the story (which begins in chapter 42) reveals, Joseph holds an even greater advantage: He recognizes his brothers, but they do not know it is Joseph before whom they grovel. Joseph does scheme and plot in a way that might have made father Jacob proud, putting his brothers through a series of contrived embarrassments. But all the way through, Joseph is never far from tears (43:30; 45:1-2). In the end, Joseph arranges the private audience where he reveals that the one they thought to be dead now stands before them. And not only that: Joseph declares that God has used the worst of their actions to preserve life.

Joseph employed his power to enact forgiveness. And from forgiveness came reconciliation and reunion.

It is this exercise of power that makes the story so surprising and unexpected. Once success and privilege come into our lives, settling scores and exacting revenge prove tempting options for many. "Don't get mad; get even" is a refrain not only heard but enacted. To forgive a person over whom you have power—a person you can demote, control, or coerce—is truly an act of grace, an act in keeping with Joseph's character. Perhaps that character of forgiveness goes back to Joseph the dreamer, whose dreams oriented him to the future. In many ways, forgiveness provides the only sure path into the future. Without forgiveness, we are tied to the past and its wrongs. Without forgiveness, either we will never get revenge on all who have hurt us or we will never make amends for all the times we have done the hurting. Forgiveness makes it possible to leave those slights and faults behind, even as it opens the way to fresh starts and renewed relationships.

For Joseph, forgiveness was the only way to piece his family back together. Joseph exercised forgiveness for the same reason he earlier exercised wisdom: to accomplish what Joseph understood to be God's purpose for his life. "For God sent me before you to preserve life"—life preserved through famine by wisdom. Life preserved through guilt by forgiveness: the opportunity for revenge met by the commitment to forgive. May Joseph teach us well.

For Meditation This Day

When I have the power and cause to punish, help me to have the grace and spirit to forgive.

*Based on "I Want Revenge" from *Peace Be with You* by Cornelia Lehn (Newton, Kans.: Faith and Life Press, 1980), 67–68.

~

Wednesday

Genesis 48:8-20   The Best-Laid Plans

*Israel stretched out his right hand and laid it on the head of
Ephraim, who was the younger, and his left hand on the head of
Manasseh, crossing his hands, for Manasseh was the firstborn.*

EVERY DETAIL HAS TO BE IN PRECISE ORDER. Every movement has to be exactly as choreographed. Every face has to
have the right look. Every posture has to be aligned just so.

Whether planning for the perfect holiday gathering of
family or arranging the ideal wedding or posing for the family
portrait photographer or staging the Broadway production, we
sometimes like to have things in order and under control. We
go to great lengths, whether through rehearsal or explicit in-
struction, to insure that all understand what is expected of
them—and what cannot be allowed.

Joseph, the administrator of Pharaoh, had years to practice
such precise planning. The discipline of not squandering
resources during years of plenty, the discipline of careful allot-
ment during years of famine: Doubtless these responsibilities
made Joseph a careful and precise manager. And now, as he
stands before the deathbed of his father, Jacob-now-Israel, to
seek blessing for his own two sons, Joseph choreographs one
more scene. Knowing his father can no longer trust his own
eyes, Joseph moves his sons like pawns on a chessboard to
insure that elder and younger receive the appropriate blessing.
Joseph even herds them close enough so their ailing grandfather doesn't even have to get out of bed. All Israel has to do is
stretch out his arms.

But like the child in the family picture who won't stand

still, or the relative whose unexpected behavior raises eyebrows at the Christmas dinner, Israel digresses from the script. Israel crosses Joseph up—literally. As the grandfather prepares to give his blessing, he crosses his arms: right hand upon the younger child, left hand upon the elder. And he gives his blessings respectively.

Now this text is not the story of an old man who didn't know his right from his left or an elder from a younger. No, this is a story of an old man who knew all too well that God worked contrary to social convention. He knew all too well the assumptions of sons who would handle all the arrangements ahead of time so as to leave nothing to chance—or grace. Israel was not always Israel: His birth name was Jacob. He knew from the inside how God might choose the one without birthright.

People like you and I might ask, So what? What do the hands, or even the words, of an elderly, dying man have to do with the future of other generations? However, Genesis is not a book of scientific cause-and-effect reasoning. It is a book of blessing and wonder. It is a book where the right hand of an aged man can be the instrument of blessing. It is a book where God chooses almost without fail the unexpected: Promise is extended to the cheating Jacob, and refuge given to the murdering Cain.

Joseph does nothing wrong in bringing his sons before Israel in their proper order. It is not as if our desire to plan and manage what comes to us in life is an offense to the Almighty. What this brief encounter reveals, however, is the freedom of God's grace to move where it will.

Sometimes grace will confirm our plans and directions in life—but not always. Sometimes grace will cross its hands and bless what and whom we did not expect. Sometimes, as this week makes clear, grace demonstrates its power for life by revealing its willingness to endure suffering and death. For the God of Jacob, whose arms cross to bless, is the God of Jesus …whose cross unfolds to bless.

For Meditation This Day

O God, keep me open to your unexpected ways, your unconsidered choices, and your unforeseen grace.

﹏

Epilogue

MAUNDY THURSDAY

Genesis 49:28-33   Burial As Hope

"Bury me with my ancestors…in the field that Abraham bought from Ephron the Hittite as a burial site."

IT WAS THE FIRST AND ONLY TIME I HELPED transport a body across the border. Irl lived across the street from us. We held his funeral at the church I served in northeast Washington. But Irl had left instructions to be buried in British Columbia. I've long since forgotten the reasons, if I ever knew to begin with. Some folks probably wondered why this old bachelor thought it made any difference where he was interred. But it made a difference to Irl. We kept his wishes for a resting place in native soil.

After learning that Joseph lived, Jacob packed up and moved —with the rest of his family—to live with his now-prominent son. Egypt, however, was not home ground. And dying Jacob would have nothing to do with a grave dug in foreign soil. So the patriarch made his wish for burial in the site purchased by Abraham (49:29-32) clear to all his children. He made Joseph swear to return his body to the tomb in Canaan, an oath his son revealed to Pharaoh in order to obtain permission to go (50:5-6).

Was an old man's wish worth the effort and the expense? The journey from Egypt to Hebron did nor represent an idyllic stroll completed in a day. The most direct route stretched close to three hundred miles, much of it through the rocky barrens of the wilderness of Shur. Providing food for such a journey for the large company recounted in Genesis 50:7-9 required a major effort. Was Jacob engaging in one last irrational bargaining session? Wouldn't a grave in Egypt suffice?

For bones, yes; for hope, no. Remember, this is Jacob, the recipient of father Isaac's blessing: a blessing whose covenant promises involved not only descendants but land. True, promised descendants surrounded Jacob's deathbed. But the land of promise remained distant. And if life went well in Egypt, Jacob's heirs might forget that land, forget the way home. So as if in rehearsal of some later homecoming and promise-keeping, Jacob plots his course—and that of his family—back to the land.

Their land. For Jacob is quite specific about where he wants his dead bones borne: to "the cave in the field at Machpelah, near Mamre, in the land of Canaan, in the field that Abraham bought from Ephron the Hittite as a burial site." Jacob designated his burial in the one corner of earth, the one tiny parcel of ground that the promise-bearers owned. It was as if Jacob considered the burial plot as a garden plot, and his entombing as planting a seed: the seed of God's promise of land; a seed that would one day break the crust and thrust sunward and bloom for the children's children's children of the faces Jacob dimly saw gathered around his deathbed.

Listen to Jacob's story this eve of the day when we remember another death, another entombment, and prepare to stand vigil again for the remarkable claim of burial as hope—hope in a promise that will be kept, hope that the children of the promise will here see and remember the grace that leads to home. Thanks be to God for the burial of Jacob and its testimony to hope!

For Meditation This Day

Do I hope as strongly as your grace gives me reason, even in the face of death? Help me to have hope; help me to give hope.

~~~

GOOD FRIDAY

Genesis 50:15-21   Good from Evil

"Even though you intended to do harm to me, God intended it for good."

MAKE NO MISTAKE. THE BROTHERS of Joseph intended, and succeeded, in doing great harm. They sold their own kin into slavery. To hide their crime, they led their father to believe that his favorite son was dead. Theirs was not a childish prank, mean-spirited but soon undone. Years of slavery and grief resulted from the harm done by their sin.

Years of guilt and fear also followed (42:21-22). Their dismay at learning their brother still lived surfaced at Joseph's initial self-disclosure. And Joseph's gracious words (45:5-8) and his ensuing provision for them in Egypt did not erase all their fear for what they had done. Jacob's death triggers lingering guilt and anxiety. Forgiven once, they cry for forgiveness again—even if it means slavery (50:15-18).

Once again in a position to unleash revenge for evil done, Joseph graciously chooses good. Their intended harm, he declares, became God's opportunity to do good. Joseph declines to play God in terms of revenge. Instead, he mirrors God's own way with him by promising to provide for his brothers. Good not only comes from evil in this story; good embraces those who did evil.

Now some may balk at the application of this story. Joseph's prosperity, they might say, makes his graciousness convenient. What if Joseph still wallowed in prison? What if he had died in the pit into which his brothers first cast him? Would the author of Genesis still be telling us that good comes from evil?

Such concerns naturally surface in a world where evil often seems to hold the upper hand while good goes unrewarded. One inner-city youth makes minimum wage by flipping hamburgers, while another rakes in an amazing salary by supplying drugs to users. Those who engage in terrorism increasingly gain our attention, while those who labor for change in quiet ways go ignored. So is Joseph's story of good from evil a pipe dream, wishful thinking on the part of those who wish the world were otherwise? Doesn't the real world grind up such grace, reducing its hope to ashes?

This day we remember another child upon whom others intended, and succeeded in doing, great harm. He too was a child sold for silver, though the price in flesh had gone from twenty to thirty pieces over the years. His robe was not returned to a grieving father, having been carefully dipped in the blood of a slaughtered goat to conceal the crime. Instead, his robe was gambled among executioners, whose very public work that day involved shedding the blood of the one whom John the Baptist had called God's lamb.

Jesus, like Joseph, offered words of forgiveness to those who intended and succeeded in doing him harm. Unlike Joseph's words, however, those words did not come from the graciousness of power restrained from taking revenge but from the graciousness of power made vulnerable through the endurance of death.

It is precisely that vulnerability that makes the story of the cross the ultimate embodiment of Joseph's affirmation of good from evil. When the crucifiers have done their worst, when life has been stripped, when no more evil can be done, Joseph's ancient words begin to softly whisper in the shadows of Golgotha and a garden tomb: "Even though you intended to do harm to me, God intended it for good." The most evil of human intentions have been fulfilled: the killing of God's beloved. And yet through that evil, God will bring grace's greatest good: our forgiveness, our healing, our life. All from a Friday grace made Good.

For Meditation This Day
Make me a seeker and doer of the good, even when the seeking and the doing seem without hope or without reward, for you are good.

~~⌒

HOLY SATURDAY

Genesis 50:24-26   Out of Egypt

*"When God comes to you, you shall
carry up my bones from here."*

SOME HAVE NOTED THAT CHILDREN tend to become like their parents. Joseph mirrors father Jacob in one aspect at his father's time of dying. Like his father, Joseph is not content for his bones to rest in foreign soil. Unlike Jacob, Joseph does not insist that those bones be transported immediately after death. Instead, he links their conveyance with hope in a future act of God's deliverance. Joseph obtains an oath that his descendants will take his bones with them when God comes to bring the people from Egypt to the land promised in covenant.

We have considered already whether dry bones know anything of their interment place. Joseph is not Ezekiel, envisioning dry bones leaping to life at God's word. But Joseph is a child of the covenant promises. Even in death, he is determined to bear witness to his trust in God's fulfillment of those promises. Genesis ends without a clear resolution of this matter. Joseph dies, to be sure. Yet the final verse leaves the situation up in the air—or perhaps better said, deep in the ground. "[Joseph] was embalmed and placed in a coffin in Egypt." Period. End of chapter. End of book. Will the oath of the Israelites be kept? Will God bring them up out of Egypt to the land sworn to Abraham and Isaac and Jacob? Genesis doesn't say. The story's conclusion awaits another day, another book.

And that is what makes the conclusion of Genesis such an apt text with which to conclude this Lenten study on the day called Holy Saturday. Today the church keeps vigil in yet another interim time. The liturgy of Good Friday has left no doubt about Jesus' fate. Like Joseph, the crucified one lies entombed.

Women prepare spices and perfumes for the final anointing that was the Palestinian equivalent of embalming. Roman soldiers stand guard before a stone-sealed cave that served for a coffin. Lent concludes on Holy Saturday with hope awaiting fulfillment, with vigils in darkness awaiting the gift of light, with the faithful waiting to see if God will indeed bring God's own out of Egypt.

Times of waiting vary. From Joseph's death to the Exodus, 400 years stretched hope to its breaking point. From 3:00 P.M. Good Friday until sometime after Holy Saturday's midnight, all creation teetered in the balance between life's power and death's hold. Even now, you and I live in the interim where life unfolds on the side of the grave that requires hope, that requires grace.

Throughout this season, we have journeyed with our spiritual ancestors in Genesis. Why? They understood what it meant to live by hope. They understood what it meant to receive grace. Whether in creation's making or Adam and Eve's clothing, whether in Cain's marking or Noah's remembering, whether in Abraham's journeying or Isaac's loving, whether in Jacob's choosing or Joseph's providing: The story remains the same. God favors the most common and unlikely of persons with the most uncommon and surprising grace. And through these persons, Genesis reveals the beginnings of God's love for you and me and all creation.

God's love will not let us go forgotten any more than it left Joseph forgotten in an Egyptian coffin, any more than it left Jesus forgotten in a garden tomb. In God's gracious remembrance we find our life and hope and home for all time to come.

For Meditation This Day
Alpha and Omega, your grace stretches from creation's beginning to hope's fruition. Remember me with grace and keep me in love.

~

Dominic Urbano

About the Author

A native of St. Louis, JOHN INDERMARK now lives in the town of Naselle in southwest Washington with his wife, Judy, and son, Jeff. The author is an ordained minister in the United Church of Christ and has served U.C.C., United Methodist, and United Presbyterian congregations over the past twenty-one years. His published writing has included adult studies and other curriculum materials for *The Inviting Word* and *Bible Discovery*, as well as devotional articles for *The Upper Room Disciplines* (1997, 1998). When not involved in writing or parish work, you may find John fly-fishing, beachcombing for agates, or watching Jeff play basketball.